RARE ELVIS

VOLUME ONE

Published by

Elvisly Yours Ltd.
P.O. Box 315
London NW10
England

Copyright © Sid Shaw 1990

ISBN 1-869941-04-7

British Library Cataloguing in Publication data

Shaw, Sid
    Rare Elvis, Volume One
    1. Presley, Elvis-Portraits, etc
    2. Singers-United States-Portraits
    I. Title
      782.42166092

First published in U.K. in 1990

Author and Editor: Sid Shaw
Reproduction & Design: Bowman Litho Ltd.
Typesetting: O'Reilly Clark Typesetting
Printed by: Stanhope Press

Editorial and design assistance by David Griffiths and Brian Savill.
Photographs from the Elvisly Yours Collection.

Rare Elvis is the third Elvisly Yours book after
Elvis A King Forever and *Elvis in Quotes* which are available
from Elvisly Yours in hardback or paperback editions.

News articles about natural health products an holistic services from across the Globe. This editio featuring:-
AAFCO STANDARDS - A Worthless Measure fc determining the Nutritional Value of Pet Foods?
Grooming with trust
The Yorkshire Essence Flower Trials
A Terrier's Holistic Recovery from Hip Surgery
Fireworks! 5 Tips For Keeping Fearful Pets Calm and much much more...

Healthful was established in 2011 with the concep of Canine Health via Nutrition, it has grown t be a source of information with regards to no only nutrition, but natural products, alternativ therapies and issues brought about by 'pet fooa and conventional medicine. In order to mak this information available to a greater number of discernin, consumers, Healthful Dog Journalzine was created.

ISBN 9781548973766

90000 >

9 781548 973766

RARE ELVIS

VOLUME ONE

Sid Shaw

ELVISLY YOURS LTD.
P.O. BOX 315
LONDON NW10
ENGLAND

LONDON • MEMPHIS • LENINGRAD

THE VERY BEST OF

No. 1
LIMITED EDITION
XMAS 1980

95p
USA $3.00

Elvisly Yours

OFFICIAL PHOTO ALBUM
AND CATALOGUE

INSIDE
PHOTO ALBUM
POSTER
FREE COMPETITION
HUNDREDS OF
MEMENTOES

ELVISLY YOURS COMMENTS

It was August 1980 just three years since Elvis had died and three years since the idea of Elvisly Yours was conceived and two short years that we had been in business. We started in the publishing business after a very humble start with a leaflet printed in 1978 when money was so short we couldn't even afford to have typesetting and everything was handwritten on a small brochure to advertise our first products, Elvis busts and plaques. The first Elvisly Yours publication for sale was to prove extremely popular, it was a full colour poster magazine. But a poster magazine could not provide the service that Elvis fans were clamouring for. In October 1980 we produced our very first copy of Elvisly Yours which was a different type of publication. It was a magazine packed with rare black and white photos and at the same time a catalogue of hundreds of Elvis souvenirs. It was the beginning of a new episode in the Elvis World and which continues to this day all over the world. Today Elvis fans in over 50 countries deal directly with Elvisly Yours.

Sadly, only American fans can't share in our success and no American fan living in the States can join our fan club, buy our souvenirs or collect our magazines because Priscilla Presley and the Elvis Estate have been suing Elvisly Yours. Elvis fans in America can join any fan club they want, buy all types of unlicensed Elvis products from the clubs and dealers but not from Elvisly Yours. The lawsuit has been going since February 1985. Amazingly, in 1982 we were supplying the Elvis Estate with Elvis souvenirs and they repeated ordering until the lawyers got greedy. They are suing us for selling Elvis souvenirs that they were buying.

At the time of writing we are still locked in dispute, under an injunction and appealing the Federal rulings of the Tennessee Court to the US Appeals Court and the case will eventually be a decision for the US Supreme Court. Meanwhile in the rest of the world we go from strength to strength and discover more and more Elvis fans from Russia to Argentina and Iceland to Abu Dhabi. Elvis is a truly international phenomena and we get letters from the most unlikely places often in strange languages and the addresses are written in a very foreign style so to reply all we can do is photocopy the address and stick it on an envelope and hope that it gets to Iran or Hungary or the Cook Islands.

Back in October 1980 we were assured that the Elvisly Yours magazine format would not work by many people and particularly by the head buyer of magazines for W. H. Smith. He told our magazine distributor it just wouldn't sell only to find that week when he went home his own son had bought a copy and loved it. But Elvisly Yours has had its downs as well and one issue was banned by the newsagent trade but more of that later. The two greatest appeals of Elvisly Yours magazines are the unique collection of photographs and the range of souvenirs available for fans to purchase. Many of the colour photographs have appeared in our two previous books *Elvis A King Forever* and *Elvis in Quotes* but we have used hundreds of black and white rare photographs. This book is the very best of those unique photos in large format and reproduced to the same excellent quality as the prevous ten years of publication. In the ten years since we first published Elvisly Yours we have kept with the same repro and printing team who have given us an excellent service. The black and white repro has been by Bowman Litho, the colour repro by Compliment Colour and the colour printing by Camden Colour with black and white printing by Stanhope Press. Only the typesetting agencies have changed over the years. Keeping the same excellent

publishing team has allowed us to maintain the highest standards and fans all over the world have always praised the high quality of our magazines in which we take great pride.

Rare Elvis is a feast of photographs and particularly *Volume One* was planned to make the reader share in this magnificent visual representation of not only the world's greatest star but one of the world's most handsome men. The attraction of Elvis is that in every photo he looks different. He has a different smile or sometimes he looks meaner or sometimes moody, has a laugh in his eyes or just love or sex or hope or joy. Each look was just *personally* for each fan. He was one helluva good looking guy and please do enjoy this wonderful collection of photographs. But this book is not just about the image of Elvis it wants to highlight ten years of all our magazines and all the stories, the fun and the sadness, the crazy Elvis inspired events and even the poems and letters which all have helped to make Elvisly Yours the best regular Elvis Presely magazine in the world.

The first ever issue was unique and shows Elvis actually holding our first Elvisly Yours magazine which showed him holding our magazine showing him holding our magazine and so on ad infinitum. It was an interesting series of photos within photographs and we thought we were very clever but alas we didn't get one letter of praise for such a unique cover so we had to find an even more eyecatching design for issue no. 2 of the first series. Our first magazine had proved so successful and we had thousands of orders for Elvisly Yours souvenirs that it finally gave us the cash flow to plan to build a statue of Elvis as a permanent memorial to him in Britain. We wanted to promote the idea that Elvis was finally coming to Britain (as a statue) and needed to find something or some concept that would be very British and would represent Britain and Elvis. Now Elvis had been in Britain and dedicated fans will know that he briefly touched down in Scotland on his way back to America by air from West Germany after his Army service. But perhaps unkown to anyone else he had secretly come over at an earlier time in his career? Now what represents Britain more than anything around the world? . . . the royal family. So the idea was created that Elvis maybe secretly met the Queen on an earlier visit and we had to have a photograph to record this historic event and give us the caption . . . "The King . . . was he in England?" with the answer "*NO*, but Elvis is coming". So that in the next magazine we could show all the fans around the world the sculptor Jon Douglas working on the life size clay model from which was sculptured a bronze statue. Little did we know what uproar would follow.

The front cover was carefully designed and I remember the repro company continually fighting to keep Elvis and the Queen apart. But I insisted they should be cheek to cheek. So a series of negatives were developed gradually giving the final proof with a clever mock-up of Queen Elizabeth side by side with Elvis and cheek to cheek . . . cheeky maybe, but a copy of the magazine was sent to the Queen and to this day she never complained or her aides. I expect if she did see the magazine she had a quiet chuckle. The photo did Queen Elizabeth proud and showed a delightful photo of her in the early years of her reign. The photo was ordered from Rex features who had the exclusive for the story which then broke in the Press after the magazine was finally published. An advance copy was sent to the various magazine distributors and also to the head buyer for W. H. Smith. They all refused to carry the magazine. Our 'King and Queen' cover was banned. Even the "GIRLIE" magazine distributors would not take our no. 2 issue of Elvisly Yours and the Queen never complained. Ten thousand magazines had been printed when we had to change the cover at short notice. In a flash we had another 30,000 magazines printed with a new cover of Elvis in his boxing outfit from "Kid

Galahad". We had thousands of magazines with the Queen on the cover that we needed to sell. The story appeared in the "People" newspaper about our Elvis magazine being banned and then the phone started to ring with fans asking how to get hold of a copy. We placed an ad with the "People" to sell the magazine. When the "People" saw the cover and even though they had ran a story and featured the banned cover they refused to accept the ad. Freedom of the Press? . . . It was okay to show the cover and write about it but we weren't allowed to advertise it in their paper. We hunted all over Fleet Street and finally the only paper willing to let us run an ad for the "King and Queen" copy of Elvisly Yours was the Daily Star. Meanwhile more papers had picked up the story and still the fans couldn't obtain a copy except from us. When the Star saw the cover they announced that we could only feature the cover in the ad with the Queen removed. We obliged and just left her crown. The Daily Star still objected so in the end we had to run an advertisement with the cover featuring Elvis and a big hole where the Queen and her crown would have appeared. Still the saga didn't end as the official body for the newagent trade then complained to the Daily Star about running the advertisement and we thought there would be a lawsuit. All these figures from the Establishment protecting our Queen who probably enjoyed the idea after a copy was sent to her with a letter of explanation. There are still some copies left of the 1981 magazine and for posterity we have in our offices a giant blow up of the cover 8 feet high by 4 feet wide.

The number 3 issue eventually came out with a full page photo of Jon Douglas working on our beautiful statue which shortly after was to collapse and poor Jon had to start all over again. The statue took seven months to complete and was finally unveiled in London by Charlie Hodge in September 1981. Alas we naively felt that a London museum would love to have a statue of Elvis donated but they all turned the idea down. The statue was on temporary display at Capital Radio when they found that it did not have a home. They organised a huge press conference with our Elvis outside Captial Radio on Euston Road and all the papers and TV were there. We were delighted because we hoped the publicity would shame one of the major London museums into accepting the statue so that thousands of people could see it. Alas, shortly after the press conference the bomb went off in the Wimpy Burger Bar on Oxford Street when the poor bomb disposal man died and that was the end of the news about our Elvis statue. That same week the Daily Mirror ran the exclusive series on the Goldman book and the following week we helped sponsor the campaign in the Daily Star called "WE LOVE ELVIS" when 23,000 fans wrote in to the Star thanking them for standing up for Elvis and attacking the smears of Albert Goldman. Over the years unusual happenings connected with Elvis have occured over and over again and deserve another book. Many of these happenings have occured with the Statue.

The Elvisly Yours Statue almost never was. Jon Douglas, the sculptor, became paralysed in his hands less than two weeks before the statue was complete. He had made the huge mould but then couldn't complete the statue. It was finished with the help of his sons and everyone at Elvisly Yours, especially David Griffiths our General Manager. Jon instructed whilst everyone helped and just the night before the unveiling the statue was in eight parts yet to be put together, cleaned and polished. Somehow everyone worked all night and somehow a miracle occurred and it was finished. I was at the beautiful halls where the statue was to be unveiled with half the staff while the other half were polishing the statue and transporting it to the unveiling ceremony. There were so many fans wanting to be present that we had to run two shows, two unveilings. Suddenly there was a call from Paul Jardine of our staff to say that the statue had been in an accident. A car had jumped the lights and the truck carrying the statue and fans and staff had to brake sharply. Everyone in the back of the truck went flying and the statue. Several people were badly hurt and had to get hospital treatment. The only damage to the statue was that the microphone was completely bent back. Some years later Billy Stanley, Elvis' step brother was to tell me that practically every show Elvis had problems with his microphone . . . a chill went down my back as I recalled the accident to the statue. If you watch "That's The Way It Is" you can see Elvis toss one microphone after the other aside as he finds problems with them.

The statue has travelled extensively and was almost arrested outside Buckingham Palace when it was felt on the way to an Exhibition at the Mall Galleries it would be nice to have a photo of the "King at the Palace". We unloaded the Statue as onlookers stared in disbelief and with the help of the Daily Mirror press photographer proceeded to take some nice shots of our Elvis at the Palace . . . photographs fit for a King. Alas, the Police Officer on duty who towered to over SIX FEET SIX didn't find our photo session at all amusing and practically arrested me and Elvis outside Buckingham Palace but it was a nice pic for the family album. The policeman must have been a Barry Manilo fan. The statue has been the length and breadth of England, Scotland and Wales and was taken to West Germany to commemorate the 30th anniversary of Elvis landing in Germany. The story was picked up all over the world and appeared on West German television, live on the radio and in all the newspapers and magazines. The statue now stands proudly in the Elvisly Yours Centre in London.

The Elvisly Yours Statue began an extensive series of shows that were to invite to Britain many of Elvis' close friends and members of his family to meet the British fans and indeed European fans have often come over expecially to Britain. Over the years Elvisly Yours have invited to Britain Harold Loyd, David Stanley, George Klein, Charlie Hodge, Richard Davis, Dee Presley, Larry Geller, Joe Esposito, Myrna and Jerry Schilling. It was Myrna and Jerry who opened officially the Elvisly Yours Centre in London on January 9th 1983. Fans from all over the world have been to visit our Centre and we used to keep a visitors book until some kind soul stole it a few years ago. What they wanted with a visitors book God only knows but if you know who stole it please let us know or perhaps the kind person would return it someday? It was a nice keepsake because of all the names of all the fans and the special guests that have visited our Centre over the years. To fans in Britain our Centre has become a shrine and many fans bring flowers, cards and write poems in memory of Elvis. Every January 8th and August 16th we host a FREE convention at our Centre which is supported by hundreds of fans and a chance for fans to meet and share their love for Elvis and in recent years the January birthday celebrations have also become a reunion for many of the fans who had gone on our Elvisly Yours Fan Club Tour to Memphis.

While many fans had the opportunity to meet people close to Elvis at our British events other fans had saved their money, in some cases for many years, to make the pilgrimage to Memphis and there had the wonderful opportunity to not only visit Graceland, see Elvis' grave and pay their respects but also to talk to many members of Elvis' family and friends who had not been to Britain. Elvis' favourite Aunt Loraine had always been a special lady to our fan club and every year came to the Airport to meet the fans and visited us at our hotel. She loved Elvis and loved the fans and especially our fans. Sadly she died shortly after our trip in 1988 and in her memory we started the Aunt Loraine Memorial Appeal to help us to continue to raise money to take to Memphis handicapped Elvis fans and fans from behind the Iron Curtain. For some years we had already had an Appeal to raise money to take

handicapped Elvis fans to Graceland that had proved an enormous success. The first Appeal started in 1984 when another fan club asked for our help, the "Today, Tomorrow and Forever Elvis Club" had decided to assist Tony Tonks, a severely disabled boy, to make his dream come true and go to Graceland. Over £4,500 was raised and Tony and his family went to Memphis. Sadly Tony died a few months later but his bravery, his love for Elvis and his tenacity influenced all the fans on the trip, Mayor Morris and the people of Memphis. Each year it has been wonderful to see how the fans on our trip, many of whom have never come into contact with handicapped people, all relate to, help, encourage and treat the handicapped equally with love and kindness. It was a tradition started by Elvis himself and which our fan club gladly continues today. After Tony's visit we took John Rowan and John Tompkins, Martin Hull, Bobby Dobson, and John Kelly. Each year the two mayors in Memphis have honoured the handicapped fans with Keys to the City and made them Honorary Citizens, the people of Memphis have opened their hearts to them and we have inspired millions of ordinary people to relate to the handicapped more positively with all the press and TV coverage that has occured. In February 1988 over 27 million people saw how John Rowan and John Tompkins had the surprise of their lives when the famous British TV programme "Surprise, Surprise" filmed the occasion when they both without any prior knowledge got their tickets and were off on our Memphis Tour the next day. It was very touching when John Rowan who is Down Syndrome asked if he could say a few words and made an impromptu speech in front of two TV camera crews and millions of viewers. It brought a tear to the eyes of millions of people and did much for the mentally handicapped in Britain. In addition to the handicapped people we have taken to Memphis we have encouraged other groups to raise money and sponsor more handicapped fans and now almost every year additional handicapped Elvis fans are sponsored by different organisations.

The death of Aunt Loraine inspired me to look further afield and make our Appeal a truly International event. At the time it was almost impossible to get anyone out of Russia and especially a rock'n'roll fan. So the Aunt Loraine Memorial Appeal was to internationalize the whole idea of our fund raising and fans all over the world combined their efforts to raise the £4,000 target. But how do you identify a big Russian Elvis fan? The Soviet Embassy was of little help and in desperation I approached the BBC World Service who said they had a big rock'n'roll programme that was broadcast each Saturday to the Soviet Union and its presenter Seva Novgorodsev may be able to help me. Indeed Seva immediately told me about a Kolya Vasin who had helped keep alive the rock'n'roll scene in Russia all those years it was banned, essentially an underground movement. So in December 1988 I spoke to Kolya and started the process that was to become on his arrival in America one of the top ten stories in the world that day. It took 11 months to get all the papers, liaise with all the necessary authorities, co-operate with the Suspicious Minds Fan Club in America who also helped with the fund-raising and to finally get Kolya out of the Soviet Union and to Britain for a week of fun, interviews and sight-seeing and then fly with our fan club to America. We called the project "Presleynost" instead of Glasnost and this simple idea to get an exit visa for a Russian Elvis fan to visit Graceland captured the imagination of not only the American media but the world's media. When we arrived in Boston we were met by Jay Gordon a local DJ and Elvis fan who had done much to notify the media and also local press and the Associated Press correspondent. The story hit the wire services all over the world and at 5.30a.m. the next morning the phone rang from a radio station in Phoenix. I said to the DJ who wanted to speak to Kolya, "how did

you know we were here?" and he said it was in every paper in America, on every news broadcast and the biggest story around. The night before we had a huge reception at the airport when two of the local TV stations, radio stations and the newspaper all turned up together with local fans, Elvis Aunt Lois, Linda Gail Lewis and her husband Bobby Memphis. Our manager in Memphis Paula Moss had worked very hard to inform the local media about our arrival and then fans on the trip could see themselves on TV on the 10 p.m. news just after they arrived in Memphis. The next day when we went to visit Graceland there were four TV crews and Kolya's visit to Graceland made the National and International TV news that day and every day for that week. Alas, I had to pay $143 to get Kolya and the handicapped fans into Graceland who even though they had been approached independently would not give complimentary tickets. They claimed they didn't know we were coming although during August had deliberately put on a free lunch for fan club presidents in America at the exact time we were holding a fund-raising event for Kolya's Appeal and in memory of Jim Kingsley. I often wonder what Priscilla Presley, Jack Soden and Barry Ward will say when they knock on those "Pearly Gates". Our Presleynost project inspired millions of people around the world to think about Elvis in a warm, positive manner, we got Graceland millions of dollars of free publicity and we united East and West in memory of Elvis. Kolya ended up by going home with 250lbs of excess baggage and a video recorder under his arm and now at the time of writing we are planning for the next bit of "Pelvisstroika" a joint campaign with the Soviet news agency "TASS" to find the No. 1 Elvis Presley of Russia. There will be a nationwide competition to find the best Elvis in Russia and the winner will accompany the Elvisly Yours Fan Club on our trip to Memphis and Graceland. He will be joined by almost two hundred Elvis fans and three radio stations from Britain who will broadcast back to Britain. The stations are Coast-AM, Xtra-AM and GEM-AM, all of which play golden oldies and a lot of Elvis. The whole tour is organised by an exciting new travel agent, Mark One Travel of Sittingbourne in Kent. It was heart-warming to see Americans go up to Kolya in the street, shake his hand, hug him and welcome him to America and that was everywhere he went in Memphis, Tupelo, Nashville and Las Vegas and even the immigration officer on his arrival in the States knew about his visit having heard it on the radio and read about it in the papers in Boston. It will be interesting to see whether our next Presleynost project surpasses the excitement of Kolya's trip and attracts even more worldwide media coverage.

We have managed to keep good stories about Elvis in the news to counteract all the garbage and over the last ten years have given hundreds of TV, radio, newspaper and magazine interviews all over the world. We even made the pages of Playboy magazine when the Elvisly Yours Elvis Presley Party was formed and fought the Chesterfield by-Election in March 1984. Many Elvis fans would have voted Elvis President particularly in the 50's if he would have stood for that office and every election Elvis Presley gets votes where in America you can write in the name of your own candidate. At a chance meeting with David Sutch, the famous Lord Sutch of the Monster Raving Loony Party, a discussion took place whereby he encouraged me to stand with my own Elvis party and bring a bit of good old rock'n'roll to the political scene in Britain which tends to be thoroughly boring. It was Lord Sutch who stood up at the Las Vegas Press Conference and said he represented a consortium who would pay Elvis £1 million for performing in Britain. In 1969 that was a great sum and sadly the deal fell through with Colonel Parker who would not give TV rights. Sutch is a huge Elvis fan and to this day Sutch remains one of the great rock'n'rollers in the pop scene regularly playing gigs all over Britain and Europe. He is even a hero in the Soviet Union to rock'n'rollers. We held the World's First Press Conference in a Fish and Chip Shop, refused to allow the Press to ask questions in our First Press Conference and instead asked them questions about Elvis which if they got the answer correct were awarded with an Elvis souvenir as a prize. We put on free gigs and played Elvis music all over town. We were invited by the Tories to coffee at the Conservative Club, to beer at the Labour Club and the Liberals invited us to tea. It was a lot of fun and brought a lot of happiness to the people of Chesterfield and as far away as Germany and Denmark. On German TV when they reported the election they played Elvis singing 'Wooden Heart' and in Copenhagen a friend Brian Jamieson of Warner Bros. was casually watching the TV news whilst on a business trip there only to see my smiling face standing next to Lord Sutch and Tony Benn when the result was announced. The Elvis Presley Party didn't beat Benn for votes but we won by a landslide of smiles . . . Elvis would have been proud. Elvisly Yours Elvis Presley Party manifesto has now become a collectors item and I treasure my own copy signed by Tony Benn with "best wishes". The Elvis Presley Estate even used the Election campaign as an issue in the lawsuit. I was put on the witness stand as a hostile witness during a hearing with no prior warning to myself, my lawyer or the judge — another delaying tactic by the Estate but I did take the stand and then was treated to some Monty Python like questions by the Estate's lawyer. One of the suggestions in my manifesto was to rename Parliament "Graceland" and he took issue with that. I said that it gave worldwide publicity to Graceland and they should have been delighted. It seems when your making so much money there is no sense of humour just a relentless greed. With Priscilla, the lawyers, and the management who run Graceland they have no humour just a fear that someone is going to take away the money they don't deserve and haven't earned. It is the magic of Elvis that brings in the dollars. I said in an earlier issue of Elvisly Yours that if Priscilla was replaced by a baboon the Elvis Estate would make just as much money and this was later confirmed by Jack Soden, Executive Director of Graceland, who said an idiot could run Graceland and still make money. It is a great pity that all the love and warmth that surrounded Graceland and the immediate environment has been replaced by fear and greed. The old shopping centre opposite the house was a lovely place where fans would meet, be made welcome by the store owners who were their friends and one could wile away the hours knowing you would always see an old face, make a new friend. Now the object is to get you in and out as quick as possible, staff at Graceland mostly resent the fans and don't know or care about Elvis and it shows.

I have tried all the time to counteract their nastiness with humour. If you don't laugh you would cry at the way they are treating Elvis' memory and his home. Since we cannot sell Elvis souvenirs in America instead we have alternative products. In 1988 we released a t-shirt and hat with the slogan "This t-shirt (hat) is not licensed by Graceland" which was featured on local TV and in the papers. We even sold souvenirs of the Queen since we couldn't sell souvenirs of the King. In 1989 the latest design was printed on both sides of the t-shirt. On the front it said "I am NOT licensed by Graceland" and on the back it said "The following are also not licensed by Graceland" and listed "Mikhail Gorbachev, George Bush, Margaret Thatcher, the State of Tennessee (yet), Jerry Lee Lewis, the Rose Bowl and possibly Queen Elizabeth II".

Fans in America were frightened to buy them. Everyone fears being sued by the Elvis Estate. I have had five years of fans in the States saying they were right behind me but alas they are fifty paces behind so we have fought the battle alone except for one or two brave souls like Sherry Daniel of California, Sue Wiegert, Suspicious Minds Fan Club and Jerry Osborne who have matched their words with deeds and their own words in fan club publications and magazines. Now we are out of Tennessee in the lawsuit the fight has just begun. I believe that good always conquers evil and so we will win in the end however long it takes.

For some fascinating reading we have included extracts of financial accounts from the Estate up until 1984. Looking closely at the statistics you can see what the Trustees were paying themselves when there was a Probate Judge to oversee the financial affairs of the Estate. Included is the value placed on the assets — the jewellery, gold records and trophies, the value of Graceland itself and you will be shocked at how low the assets were valued. Why was Elvis' jewellery only valued at less than $5,000? In 1982 legal bills for the Estate were in excess of $800,000 and yet thereafter these bills dropped each year but then the Estate was allowed to operate Graceland as a private company and that is where I believe are hidden all the millions of dollars of expenditure for the Trustees, lawyers, executive directors, business managers and all the other vultures. It would be mind-boggling to compare these original accounts with current accounts. The Estate is always boasting how much money they are making for Lisa (or themselves in enormous fees and salaries). The Graceland operation alone probably turns over in excess of $12 million a year and a lot of that should be profit. I wouldn't mind betting that the difference between gross profit and nett profit is phenomenal and way above normal business levels. After all Priscilla has to pay herself not only as Trustee but also as President of Elvis Presley Enterprises . . . she is in trust of herself after the probate judge disappeared suddenly from the scene in 1985. Lisa signed away her inheritance until she is 30 and God knows what will be left if and when she ever gets her hands on Graceland. One day all will be revealed, let us hope sooner rather than later.

Ten years of Elvisly Yours magazines has been fun, exciting, exasperating, soul destroying and quite marvellous. We have had some good times, some great times, sad times, silly times and lots of aggravation trying to keep thousands of fans all over the world happy whilst keeping the magazine going and the Elvisly Yours Centre open while continually being attacked by Priscilla Presley and the Elvis Estate and Todd Slaughter but we are still there and planning for the next ten years. You can't keep a good man down or a good Elvis fan club. To help you savour these ten years we have put together a compilation of photographs, stories, special events, letters, quizzes . . . the very best of Elvisly Yours. But there hasn't been space to include everything so we have called our book "Rare Elvis, Volume One" and in Volume Two and Three we will hope to complete our task. Enjoy this book, buy a copy for a friend and above all keep on rockin' and lovin' Elvis.

Elvisly Yours,

Sid Shaw

This book is dedicated to all the Elvis fans in America who for many years have been denied the right to buy, read and cherish the best Elvis Presley magazine in the world, "Elvisly Yours".

THE KING

AT THE PALACE

No. 2
LIMITED EDITION
SPRING 1981

95p
USA $3.00

THE KING...
was he in England?
page

Elvisly Yours

**OFFICIAL PHOTO ALBUM
AND CATALOGUE**

INSIDE
PHOTO ALBUM
POSTER
FREE COMPETITION
HUNDREDS OF
MEMENTOES
FREE SKETCH

Jon Douglas the sculptor working on the original clay model in 1981.

CHESTERFIELD GOES ELVIS

Adding weight to the Alliance fight

By Jane Stapleton

POLITICS became a weighty business in Chesterfield as the Liberal-SDP Alliance wheeled in 28-stone MP Cyril Smith as a vote and eye-catcher.

Mr. Smith, Rochdale's heavyweight representative met Pressmen at the Party's Chesterfield headquarters and then it was out into the streets to meet the more important public and electors.

There were no problems in mistaking Mr. Smith for anyone else as he strolled around the market square, attracting bemused looks.

Meanwhile, on the other side of town, there was a Press conference with a difference — with Pressmen being asked the questions by the candidates.

Screaming Lord Sutch of the Monster Raving Loony Party and Sid Shaw of the Elivisly Yours Elvis Presley Party, created their own alliance and offered the media some light entertainment with a quiz show.

The two said they had been scouring the streets of Chesterfield, but found more candidates for other parties than voters.

On election night they plan to hold their own victory celebration and count at the Aquarius night club and then, more as an after thought, they will move on to the Goldwell Rooms for the "unofficial" count.

Harmony between the latest party alliance.

Elvis' memory lives on with Sid Shaw.

Benn is voters' favourite

TWO opinion polls show ony Benn still well ahead in the Chesterfield by-election.

Mr. Benn's lead has been clawed back slightly by the SDP-Liberal Alliance, according to the Network Intelligence poll for Central Television.

And an NOP in today's Daily Mail shows Mr. Benn with 48 per cent support compared to 27 per cent for the SDP-Liberal Alliance, 23 per cent for the Tories and 2 per cent for the others.

According to NOP only 11 per cent of voters reckoned that they might still change their minds.

Chesterfield By-Election

photographs: Chris Lawton

Lord Sutch — "confident of victory."

Chipping in with some laughs

Two by-election candidates really were fishing for votes on Tuesday — when they held the world's first ever press conference in a fish and chip shop!

Lord Sutch and Sid Shaw of the Elvis Presley Party pulled out a netful of fishy puns at the Pisces fish and chip shop in their campaign to put Maggie in her 'plaice.'

Sid presented codpieces for Mrs. Thatcher's "emasculated MPs" and set several sprats to catch the mackerels.

On his victory, Sid emphasised there would be a ban on all fish sold with the exception of rock. And, of course, his party would make sure they had plenty of sole.

Such and Shaw in their 'New Alliance' were confident their popularity was 'skating' ahead and there were plans in progress for their Victory Celebration party after the count.

To complete the aquatic theme — it took place at the Aquarius nightclub!

Frying to hold your attention . . . Screaming Lord Sutch holds the world's first chip shop press conference.

SUTCH FUN AT THE POLLS

by Lynda Murdin in Chesterfield

WHAT could be called an Unholy Alliance of candidates in the by-election here, looks set to poll a record number of votes.

Canvassing returns show that the teaming of seasoned campaigner Lord Sutch (Monster Raving Loony Party Last Stand) and Mr Sid Shaw (Elvisly Yours) could divert some 500 votes away from the main parties.

And Lord Sutch, who is not as loony as he pretends and possibly less loony than one or two mainstream candidates, is hosing more of the record fourteen fringe representatives will join him in a loosely based coalition.

"I can honestly say that I have met more candidates here than I have voters," said Lord Sutch today revealing that a new issue in his manifesto demands votes for pets.

Among others bringing a bizarre touch to a crucial by-election is a candidate of the Official Acne Party. No one here has spotted him yet.

There is also Mr Jitendra Nim Bardwaj (Yoga and Meditation) who makes a point of not disturbing voters' karma with loud speakers and political razzmatazz.

Mr Thomas Layton, a pensioner from Hove (Spare The Earth) won £5000 on a Premium Bond and was made aware of environmental issues by a radio programme the very same day.

It is the proposed raising of the deposit to £1000 that makes this probably the loonies' last stand.

But Lord Sutch—who went to a great deal of trouble to gain his title while Mr Benn had problems losing his—intends to go out in style.

Various luminaries of the Loony Party will be travelling to Chesterfield — Tarquin Blowciutlbarrel, Pete the Pub, Flying Officer Kite, Legendary Lonnie and Wally Wolly among them.

He plans rock 'n roll political meetings, and he and Mr Shaw, both resplendent figures in this staid town, are so confident of victory they plan a celebration party on March 1—before the official result is announced.

Side-splitting

Screaming Lord Sutch — veteran of nearly as many elections as Tony Benn — and his buddy Sid Shaw of the Elvisly Yours Elvis Presley Party are more likely to be splitting sides than votes.

They held an impromtu press conference in the road outside the town hall last week.

And while Sid Shaw sweetened up the Press by handing out sticks of Elvis Presley rock, Screaming Lord Sutch outlined his Monster Raving Loony Party's policies.

He also had a word of warning for the Prime Minister over plans to raise the deposit for elections from £150 to £1,000.

"If the deposit is raised I will personally go to Mark Thatcher and ask for the money. I will ask him because his mother is stopping me from standing," he declared.

Sid Shaw's message to the Government was: "There are more Elvis fans than Mrs. Thatcher fans in Chesterfield."

'Comic' Sun

And Mr. Shaw's policies? "We will abolish rates because no-one likes paying ,them and we will replace them with a tax on Cliff Richard records."

LET'S HAVE A PARTY : Lord Sutch and Sid Shaw show that politics doesn't have to be taken seriously.

Standard Pictures: COLIN DAVEY

Big noises : " Lord " Sutch and Sid Shaw canvassing yesterday

VOTE ELVIS

SID SHAW, fighting the Chesterfield by-election for the Elvisly Yours Elvis Presley Party, has some interesting policies.

For instance:

★ Parliament to be renamed Graceland.

★ Training scheme to teach Chesterfield bellringers to play Crying in the Chapel.

★ Mayor of Chesterfield to wear white jumpsuits and, if female, always to carry a teddy bear.

★ Replace policemen's boots with Blue Suede Shoes to make it less painful for Greenham Women, strikers and young people.

★ Abolish rates and replace by a special tax on Cliff Richards records.

Mr. Shaw — gaptoothed but sharp-brained (the opposite of many politicians) launched his 61 point manifesto yesterday at

Stephen McClarence
Sheffielder

Chesterfield's White Swan Hotel. He shared his platform in an upstairs room — still strewn with Christmas streamers — with Lord David Sutch of the Monster Raving Loony Party Last Stand.

The pair of them have formed the New Alliance and are planning a trip down a coal mine to launch their coal-ition. Much of what follows is similarly awful but true.

Lord Sutch, awesome in spangled lurex leopardskin tights and top hat, is an old hand at the election game. He has fought ten campaigns,

standing against Harold Wilson, Margaret Thatcher (who liked his clothes) and, as if by magic, Tony Benn — or Anthony Wedgwood Benn, as Viscount Stansgate had just become in August 1963. "But so is Michael Foot's."

His name has been linked with many of the great figures of British political life. "His hair is rather long," remarked the Evening Standard in August 1963. "But so is Michael Foot's."

Lord Sutch — no longer Screaming — wears his hair rather shorter now, gives occasional concerts, and pur-

sués policies loony enough to include Repatriation of the Normans, and serious enough to include Votes at 16, a People's TV channel, and DIY centres for the unemployed.

Sutch and Shaw — a former Ministry of Transport economist turned giftware retailer — say they are desperate to meet the voters of

Lunatic fringe? What about the lunatic hat as worn by Lord Sutch, with Sid Shaw.

Chesterfield. So far, they have met only candidates and journalists.

They met a few more journalists yesterday as, surrounded by Elvisiana, they condemned the increase of the parliamentary election deposit to £1,000. "Margaret Thatcher is going to nationalise Parliament," said Sutch.

Shaw announced that

awarded a single orange Elvis sock for correctly guessing that the song It's Now Or Never referred to Tony Benn. Only one sock? "With Kinnock in charge," said Shaw. "The Labour Party hasn't got a Foot to stand on."

"The loonies are going to come out of the closet and vote for us," forecast Sutch. "Our main rival are the Official Acne Party, but we haven't spotted them yet."

And so it could go on. About Lord Sutch's plan to rent out space on the top of his hat for a flashing light, sponsored by the University of Oman to guide young men lost in the Sahara Desert.

About his Lordship's second thoughts about his plan to straighten out the Crookes Spire. "I've taken so much stick about it that I'm going to leave it as it is," he said.

he was standing on behalf of Elvis Presley "because obviously he can't stand himself," and then detailed the novel form the Press conference would take:

"We're going to play you Let's Have a Party for five minutes — it's our theme tune — and then we're going to ask you questions."

I was personally

buildings in Chesterfield crooked to match it."

About the nuclear question. "With all the weapons that exist, you could blow the world up many times. We think once is enough."

About the proposed Chesterfield franchise for jellied eels and the next press conference, in the Pisces Fish and Chip Bar: "A world exclusive."

But it's enough to quote Sid Shaw's manifesto. It says his party aims "to bring happiness and pleasure to the Chesterfield electorate and future electorates in what otherwise would be dull, stge managed affairs."

Outside, in the windy Market Place, as the media waited and waited for colossal Liberal Cyril Smith to shoehorn himself out of a very large car and be mobbed by TV people, it looked rather as though Sid Shaw had a point. Sutch is life.

ROCKING THE BOAT : The Loony Party's Lord Sutch and the Elvis Presley candidate. Sid Shaw, at the count

THE *Elvisly Yours* CENTRE

The Elvisly Yours Centre was officially opened on January 9th, 1983 b[y] Jerry and Myrna Schilling.

ELVISLY YOURS FAN CLUB KEEPS ON GROWING.

Our fan club keeps on growing and will reach 1500 members by January 8th 1985. Keep supporting us and keep rocking with Elvis at your local branches around the country. Read our fan club news page for more details. Join now if you haven't joined.

May 1984

SUNSHINE COACH TO BE NAMED IN MEMORY OF ELVIS?

If enough money can be raised by the Elvis[ly] Fan Club through our Birthday Show and asso[ciated] fund raising effort then a Sunshine Coach w[ill be] named in memory of Elvis and will be decorated [with] Elvis Artwork. Sunshine Coaches are seen up [and] down the country transporting children here, the[re] and everywhere. It will be a great honour for our Fa[n Club] [and] a very prominent way to promote Elvi[s if we raise] enough money. [The] [C]lub will add to [the Sun]shine Coach.

ELVIS IN CANADA

George Klein and Joe Esposito hosted a special Elvis Birthday Show in Niagara Falls for the Canadian fans. About 500 fans participated over a three day event which also included a visit to Mike Moons Elvis museum in Niagara.

Hospital dedicated in Memphis to Elvis

The Presley Trauma Center was dedicated on August 15th in front of thousands of fans and dignatories in Memphis. At last Memphis is beginning to recognise its most famous son with the help of the Elvis Presley International Memorial Foundation.

The Elvis Presley Memorial Trauma Centre will open on November 10 as the only Level 1 Trauma Center in the Mid-South. The Presley Trauma Center will open in conjunction with the renaming of the [Regional] Memphis Hospital to the Regional [center at] Memphis, or THE MED [The] [Tr]auma Center is a [one of the most sophisticated ...operating]

LARRY GELLER IN BRITAIN

Larry Geller was in Britain in early October and gave [an] intervie[w]

GRACELAND IN LONDON

Graceland Enterprises had a stand at the 'World Travel Market' in London in December. The show is essentially for the travel trade. There was an excellent response by the Travel Trade to the Graceland stand and many new contacts were made with tour operators who are being encouraged to include a visit to Graceland on their American itineraries.

Ken Brixey (Marketing Director) was the Graceland representative and was highly delighted with the response. It was nice to meet Ken again and hear of all the fabulous plans for Graceland. The shopping centre has been bought by Graceland and will eventually be redeveloped with beautiful gardens where the car park now stands. Graceland will have a shop in the centre, this year, [and the] 'Million Dollar Toy' museum.

Original film poster from Charro adjacent to 11½ft. high photo of Elvis.

The all Elvis jukebox flan[ked] photo of E[lvis]

EXCLUSIVE: ELVIS ON VIDEO WITH ROLLING STONES

Yes, it's true Elvis is appearing on video with the Rolling Stones. Mick Jaggers' greatest ever regret was that he never met ELVIS but now he has. You can see ELVIS with the Rolling Stones on their new video "REWIND" available in August. How? The Rolling Stones loaned the Elvisly Yours Statue to feature extensively throughout their filming of "REWIND". Look out for "REWIND" in the shops soon.

Graceland presents 6 copies of ELVIS AT GRACELAND for Tony Tonks appeal plus personal copy autographed by Ken Brixey to Sid Shaw.

ABOUT THE SCULPTOR......

Jon Douglas is an eminent member of the Society of British Sculptors, being on the Council of this world renowned Society.

Over the many years Jon Douglas has been a portrait sculptor he has some outstanding achievements. Stanley Kubrick chose him from all sculptors to produce an exact sculptural replica of the Moon in the h[is] film '2001'. The work took over six months to complete. Mr Dougl[as] produced works on the Beatles, Pope Paul, Pope John, Churchill, Er[ic] John F Kennedy, Bobby Charlton, Harry Saltzman's children (prod[ucers of] Bond films), Spencer Tracy, Bobby Moore, Georgie Best and produc[er] Eamonn Andrews on 'What's My Line', also Peter Sellers and many [...] [all] over the world.

— where he undertakes ma[...]
[...]own char[...]
pear. H[...]

VOTE ELVIS

News of the Elvisly Yours Elvis Presley Party reached all around the globe with many countries playing Elvis music when reporting th[e] Chesterfield-by-Election o[n] radio and television. Since th[en]

King & Queen

Readers may already have heard about Elvisly Yours photo album and catalogue No 2 being 'banned' by the newsagent trade for showing a picture of Elvis with Queen Elizabeth II. Because of this, Elvisly Yours replaced the offending pictures with a shot from 'Kid Galahad'.

'Daily Star', but th[e] Queen had to be rubbe[d] out before publication.

This rar[e] collectors item is still available in very limited supplies, so make sure of your copy by ordering one now! The Daily Star was the only National daily paper to take our ad in any form,

PRESS RAVES ABOUT STATUE

The "Elvisly Yours" statue has been in the papers recently. The London *New Standard* carried a half-page picture and story on Wednesday 8th July. Also in London, the *Weekender* featured a large story on Elvisly Yours, and the statue. Regional papers also featured the press release and official preview photo. Most [...]

By the middle of August several papers will have run stories on Elvis as this commemorates the fourth anniversary of his tragic passing, lets hope they concentrate on the truth and not print sordid lies.

Freddie Starr wearing the Hawaiin belt as presented to him by the Elvis fans of Stoke, December 1980. Freddie seen with Al at the pre-recording of the Parkinson show.

The term "trauma" is a stranger to [...] trauma kills more than 150,000 [...] [It] is the third largest [aft]er heart disease and [...]

GOLDMAN . . .

The saga of the Elvis book by Albert Goldman continues. The latest news from Memphis is that Goldman has been forced to change his 'phone number. His address is 240 Central Park South, Apartment S-1, New York City, New York 10019, USA. Drop him a line and say what you feel about his book!

Meanwhile, Lamar Fyke, the man who supplied Goldman with the 'information' has disappeared after his wife had left him. No-one has yet been able to trace Lamar and there are many people who would [...] [like] to tell him what they [...]

charges): Ann Pitrone (assistant editor) 212-489-6804. Their address is 1221 Avenue of the Americas, New York 10020, USA. One true Elvis fan has been crusading in the Norfolk area to save Elvis' name. He is Barry White, who many will remember as the host at the statue unveiling. Barry has been visiting booksellers and wholesalers in his area and has succeeded in getting the book withdrawn from sale in many places. Why not do something positive and follow Barry's example ... and help keep Elvis' good name and memory ALIVE. Well done Todd Slaughter for [... ...] for Elvis in a recent Todd

ELVISLY YOURS GOES INTERNATIONAL

Elvisly Yours has now set up a permanent office in Memphis, Tennessee. The office in Memphis is run by Bena Watkins. In April, 1979 Elvisly Yours was formed with the business run from a private garage making busts of Elvis. Now just over three years later British made Elvis souvenirs from Elvisly Yours are sold all over the world, even in Memphis, Tennesse. All the gift shops opposite Graceland now stock Elvisly Yours mementoes and even Graceland. With an international set up in Memphis Elvisly Yours will be able to buy the latest souvenirs from America whilst supplying fan clubs and traders in Germany, Holland, Belgium, Denmark, Sweden, Norway, Switzerland, Brazil, Italy and even Dubai, as well as fans all over the world.

A rare photo of Goldman interviewing Elvis for his bo[ok]

Elvisly Yours Birthday Party Around The World

Our Super Elvis Birthday Party with Larry Geller went all around the world as well as TV coverage in Britain. The show was filmed by Brazilian TV, TV-AM and ABC have obtained copies of the film for broadcast in America. Also Breakfast TV featured the cake and Elvisly Yours Centre on Monday, January 9th. Photos of the cake appeared on January 8th in the Memphis paper and all over America. Elvisly Yours are keeping the name of Elvis in the headlines where h[e] belongs.

ELVIS HELPS KID COURAGE

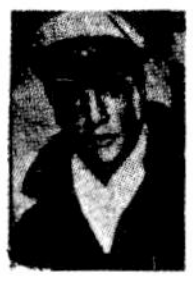

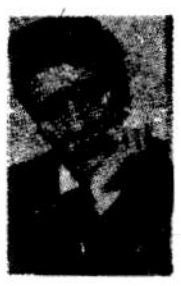

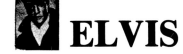

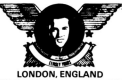

ELVIS NEWS
LONDON, ENGLAND

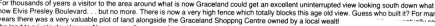

Germany honours Elvis

Not only did Germany recently honour Elvis Presley with a special Elvis postage stamp but on October 1st in Germany there will be huge remembrance celebrations for the 30th Anniversary of Elvis arriving in Germany for his army service. The event will be a major media occasion with all the fans uniting with major business to put on many Elvis related activies throughout Germany and particularly in Bremer Haven and Bad Nauheim.

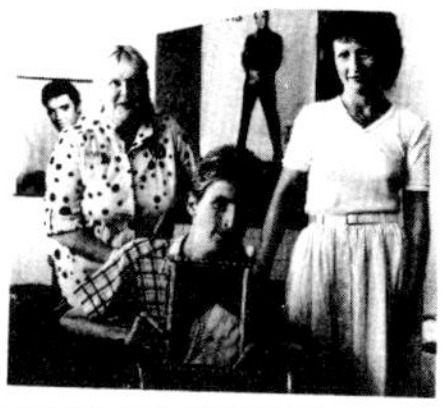

Welcome to the new Berlin Wall in Memphis

For thousands of years a visitor to the area around what is now Graceland could get an excellent uninterrupted view looking south down what is now Elvis Presley Boulevard. . . but no more. There is now a very high fence which totally blocks this age old view. Guess who built it? For many years there was a very valuable plot of land alongside the Graceland Shoppng Centre owned by a local wealt... the land to private developers. Now a marvellous new shopping centre has been ... magnificent stores an... Kentucky Fried Chicken, a brand new hotel at very reasonable prices, a carava... can't see ... because THE GRACELAND MANAGEMENT put up a fence ... fence that ... should be torn down. It is an eyesore ... ECENT PI... THEIR HARD EARNED MONEY AND ... OF GF... Graceland and get them to tear the fenc... ation to ... private stores, just in case they lose a fe... is reall... believed. Eventually they will probably ... he gur... Fortress. . . oh, oh, what would Elvis thin... h hom...

ELVIS ROCK rocks America

Americans are rocking and rolling over the latest Elvisly Yours discovery "KING ROCK" rock. They believe the name Presley goes ... the rock ca...

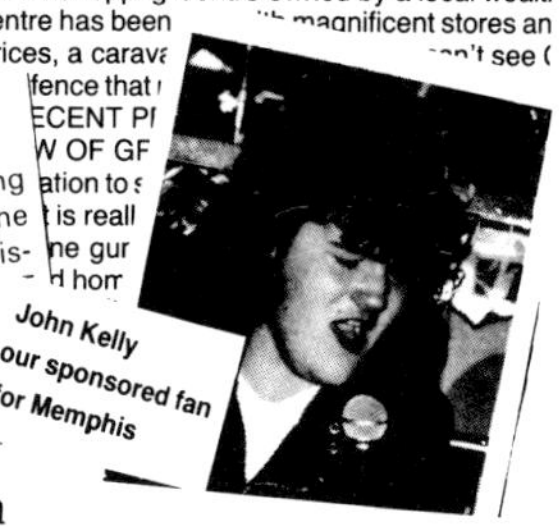

John Kelly our sponsored fan for Memphis

PRESLEYNOST OPENS THE DOOR TO A BETTER ELVIS WORLD

Already things are starting to change in Russia about Elvis. For the first time ever there was a positive and major feature on Elvis Presley in the Soviet papers, an Elvis record was released and bigger and better things are planned for 1990. Kolya Vasin is the pioneer of exciting new developements and his dream after his visit to Graceland is to open a rock'n'roll club/museum in Leningrad. All he has is one room which acts as the centre of the rock'n'roll world in Russia. We are going to see if it possible for Kolya to sell his artwork in the West to raise money for his Rock'n'Roll Centre so look out for details in our next issue of Elvisly Yours and meanwhile admire the ...ic centrespread. It is hard to imagine that there are millions of ...ans all over Russia, all crying out for more information on the ...

Are You Lonesome Tonight?

Britains top playwright Alan Bleasdale's new play starts officially on May 14th at the Liverpool Playhouse. The opening night was sold out months ago. There has been a mixed rece... tion to the news that Martin Shaw (the popular star of the T... series "The Professionals") is to be Elvis. The play will be sellout. Alan Bleasdale is a big Elvis fan. After seven years wanting to write his ELVIS play he has finally taken the plun... After leaving Liverpool the play will go to Birmingham, Brist... Leeds and Wolverhampton. For details of tickets etc at Liverp... contact "Liverpool Playhouse" ...illiamson Square, Liverpool, 1El Tel: 051-709 8363.

Tell The Truth

Sid Shaw and London Weekend TV have just completed filming a TV show for Channel 4 called "Tell the Truth". Sid was ... other people who were making out that they were also S... and the idea of the programme is that a panel of people ha... questions to try and find out who the real Sid Shaw is. Loo... this programme which is being screened later in the ye... deliverately had Sid Shaw wear a suit and another guest as Lookalike to confuse the panel.

Kolya Vasin

Kolya is a legend in Russia. He is 43 years old and has been an Elvis fan since 1958 when he first heard Elvis in the Soviet Union. Remember Elvis Presley was banned and was taboo and it took two years before many Russians first heard Elvis. Kolya is known throughout Russia because he has an open house and anyone can come in day or night and ...en to his music collection on Elvis, rock'n'roll and the ...atles. Sadly Kolya has only ONE Elvis record and all the ...st of his Elvis music is on tape b... that when I ...

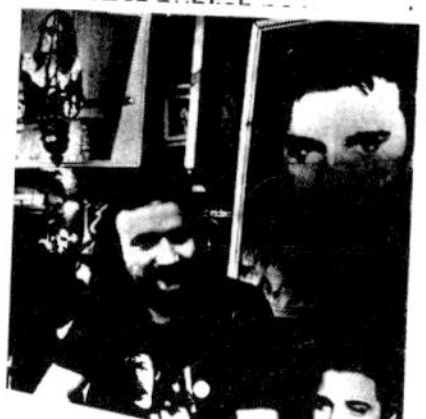

CAPITAL GOLD GOES ELVIS

Randall Lee Rose has been hosting a superb Elvis hour every Saturday on Capital Radio 1548AM between 5 p.m. and 6 p.m. It is the first time that a major radio station has devoted a regular slot to 100% Elvis music and Randall has built up a ...

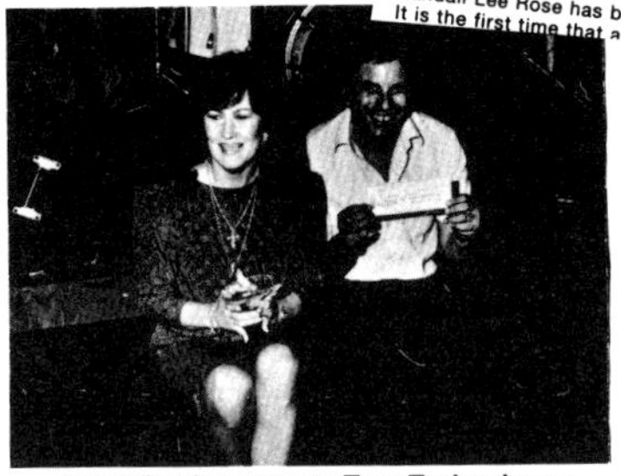

Patsy Presley presents Tony Tonks cheque to Sid Shaw at Stage '45

Britain Welcomes Gary and Willie of Memphis

Willie Johnson and Gary Chalmers became Kings of England on their exchange visit to London to tie-in with the Elvisly Yours Handicap Appeal. Everyone tre... like Royalty and they experienced all aspects of ... from Fish and Chip dinner in Hackney to tea at th... House with the Lord Mayor of London. ... policemen, firemen, taxi drivers, soldiers, an M... Mayor of London and the Mayor of Colchester, J...

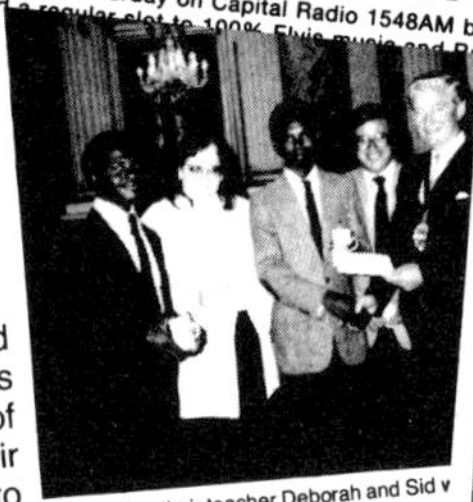

Gary, Willie, their teacher Deborah and Sid v...

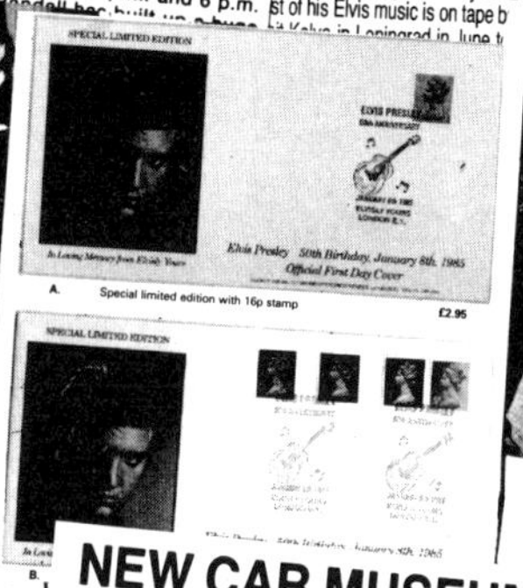

SPECIAL LIMITED EDITION
Elvis Presley 50th Birthday, January 8th, 1985 Official First Day Cover
A. Special limited edition with 16p stamp
£2.95
SPECIAL LIMITED EDITION

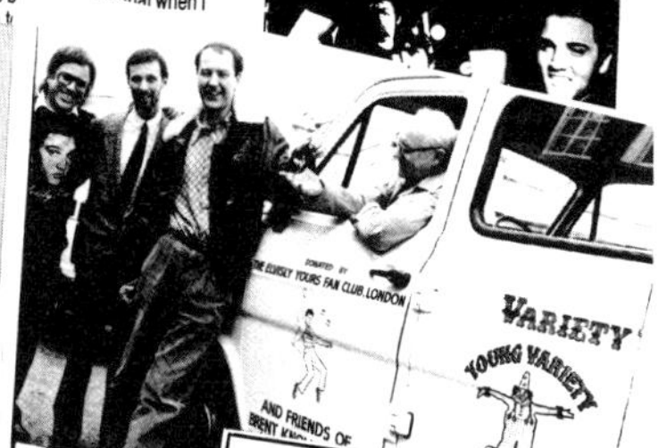

THE ELVISLY YOURS FAN CLUB LONDON
VARIETY
YOUNG VARIETY
AND FRIENDS OF BRENT KIDS

SPECIAL OLYMPICS AND RUSSIAN APPEAL IN MEMPHIS

Dr Ed Franklin has kindly provided his night club for FREE to promote a Special Olympics Appeal in memory of Jim Kingsley and as a fund raiser for US fan clubs to get Kolya Vasin to visit Graceland. Ed is the owner of Bad Bob's/Vapor Club on Brooks Road near Graceland and the ... competition fro... with a barbecu... the meal is $4.9... ould get along t... olya Vasin and ... the first eve... etition.

NEW CAR MUSEUM AT GRACELAND A SUCCESS

It took 12 years but at last Graceland have put all those beautiful cars in a museum. For years I complained that the pink Cadillac, Stutz and other histo... were being destroyed by the elements being left in the rain, frost, snow and ... fact the pink Cadillac was almost white with rust all over it. Why it took twelv... to take the simple decision to protect the cars beats me, but now they have ... and are in an excellent new museum. But of course, now you have to pa... these cars whereas before they were included in the general admission pr... sad note about this new museum is that as you enter the museum you are cc... with a massive photo of Priscilla Presley. As Trustee for the Estate it is ... flaunt herself. Fans and the public visit Gracelend to see the image of I... Priscilla. Now the cars are given the right setting for their historic significanc... years to late, but better late then never.

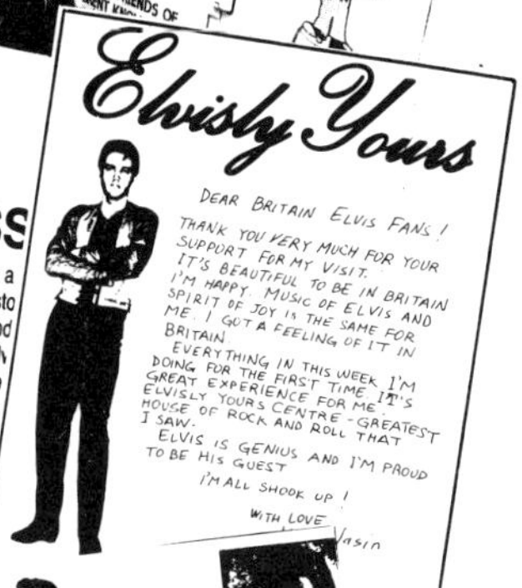

Elvisly Yours
DEAR BRITAIN ELVIS FANS!
THANK YOU VERY MUCH FOR YOUR SUPPORT FOR MY VISIT.
IT'S BEAUTIFUL TO BE IN BRITAIN
I'M HAPPY. MUSIC OF ELVIS AND SPIRIT OF JOY IS THE SAME FOR ME. I GOT A FEELING OF IT IN BRITAIN.
EVERYTHING IN THIS WEEK I'M DOING FOR THE FIRST TIME. IT'S GREAT EXPERIENCE FOR ME. I SAW ELVISLY YOURS CENTRE - GREATEST HOUSE OF ROCK AND ROLL THAT ELVIS IS GENIUS AND I'M PROUD TO BE HIS GUEST.
I'M ALL SHOOK UP!
WITH LOVE
Vasin

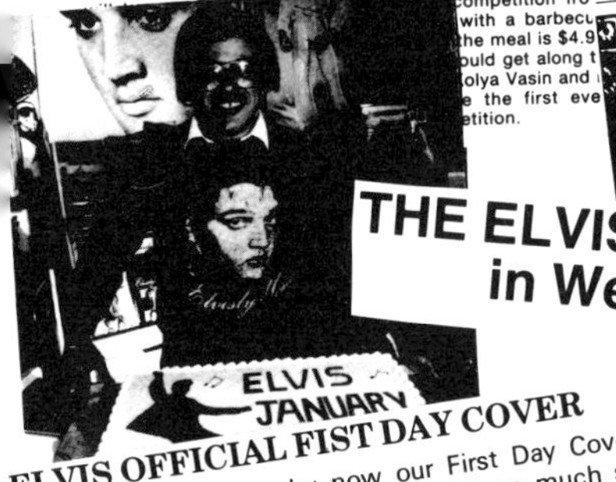

ELVIS
JANUARY

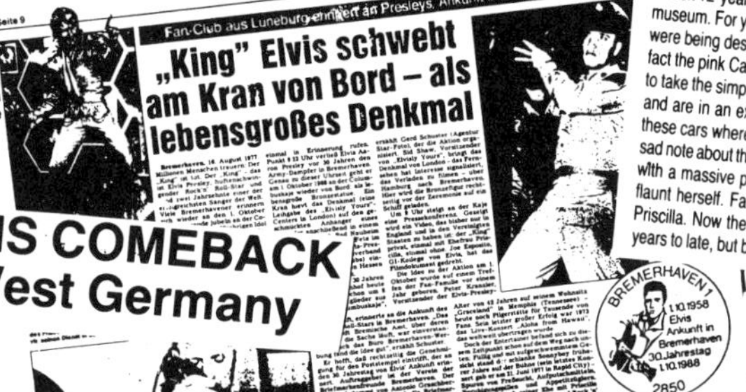

Fan-Club aus Luneburg ... an Presleys Ankunft in Bremerhaven vor 30 ...
„King" Elvis schwebt am Kran von Bord – als lebensgroßes Denkmal

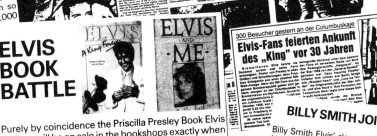

THE ELVIS COMEBACK in West Germany

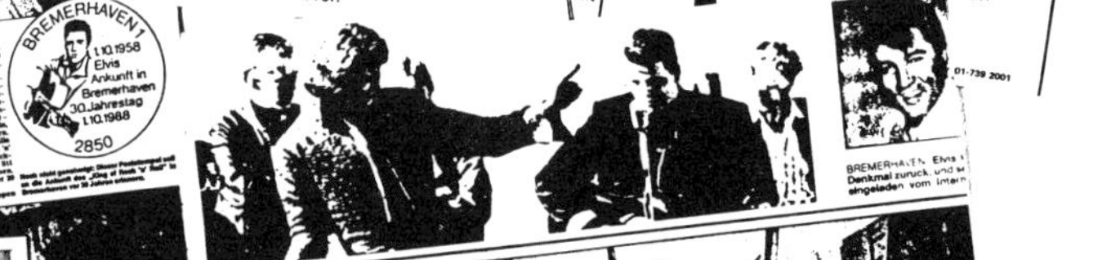

BREMERHAVEN
1.10.1958
Elvis Ankunft in Bremerhaven
30 Jahrestag 1.10.1988
2850

ELVIS OFFICIAL FIRST DAY COVER

As you will all know by now our First Day Cover caused a sensation around the world, so much so that the Post Office had to send a Telex to 29,000 (yes twenty nine thousand) local post offices i... ing conterstaff that the Elvis Presley First Day ... was only available through Elvisly Yours, giv... telephone number and address as a res... switchboard was jammed for days. See elsew... ...news of new edition...

ELVIS BOOK BATTLE

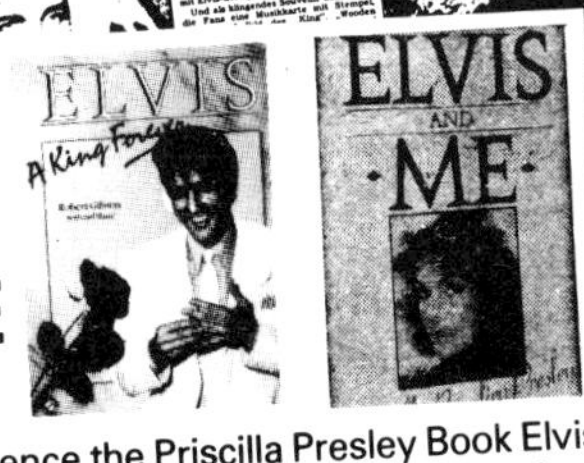

ELVIS A King Forever
ELVIS AND ME

Purely by coincidence the Priscilla Presley Book Elvis and me will be on sale in the bookshops exactly when our first book Elvis, A King Forever goes on sale. With our book, beautifully written with TLC by Rob Gibson, there will be in store displays of "I LOVE ELVIS" with special display books for our book and window displays in 50 major bookshops around Britain. Furthering the coincidence is the design of both book covers include the same STYLE of print for ELVISin the same position for each book and with additional red lettering. Make sure every bookshop in your town stocks "Elvis, A King Forever" and Smiths and Menzies. We hope that our first ever book will become the collectors book for ELVIS fans. The publishers are Blandford Press whohave heavily promoted the book to the booktrade and are sponsoring our Nationwide ...

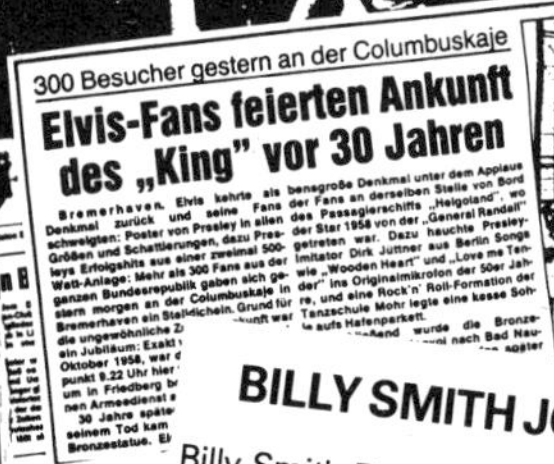

300 Besucher gestern an der Columbuskaje
Elvis-Fans feierten Ankunft des „King" vor 30 Jahren

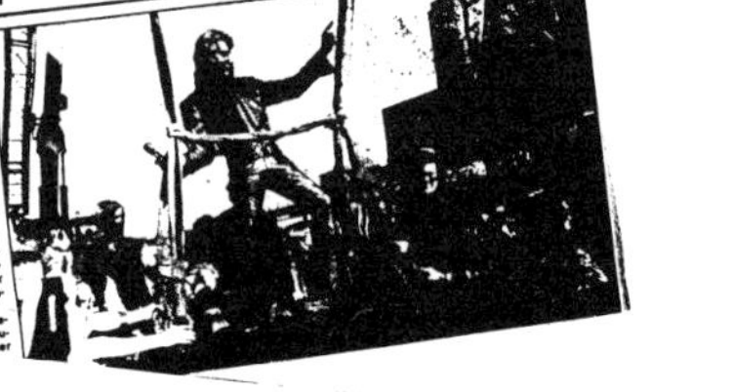

Graceland Lawyers Want to Deny Sid Freedom of Speech in America

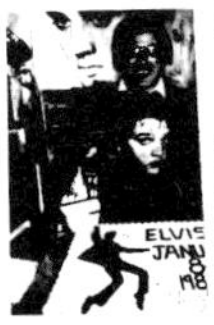

The lawyers for the Elvis Estate don't want Sid Shaw to ... present at his own defence as they say he will use t... evidence to tell the fans all the secrets about the finances ... the Elvis Estate. Until recently anyone could go down ... the Memphis Probate Court and see exactly where all th... revenue came from and went to, for eight years in fac... Now why should everything be private? It's nice to thin... Barry Ward and his crew think so highly of our tiny Elvisl... Yours magazine as if we have some sort of media powe... They even copied two pages of our editorial and put ther... forward in their defence of denying Sid his Freedom c... Speech. Apparently the Elvis Estate lawyers thin... somehow we will ridicule them by being present at th... deposition of Priscilla Presley and Joseph Hanks. What d... they think Sid is ... during cross exar... a major Federal I... of heartache anc... only ridicule is se... Estate lawyers ar...

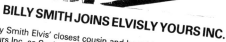

BILLY SMITH JOINS ELVISLY YOURS INC.

Billy Smith Elvis' closest cousin and best friend has joined Elvisly Yours Inc. as Senior Vice President. Billy was with Elvis all his life and was the 'kid brother'. Billy spent 18 hours each day by Elvis' side for the last two years of his life and is highly respected by all of Elvis' friends, family and especially the fans in America. Billy Smith will help promote Elvisly Yours to grow and prosper and spread the word about Elvis. We will start to offer the same excellent ... American fans as we offer in Engl... of this new...

THE WORLD'S FIRST ELVIS CHINESE RESTAURANT

If you are down the Old Kent Road in S.E. London then you are in for a surprise because the best Chinese Restaurant in South London is also a mecca for Elvis fans . . . you can eat your Peking Duck to the music of Elvis courtesy of Paul Chan. Paul is from Hong Kong and is a big Elvis fan and a restaurateer. He thought of the great idea of singing Elvis songs in his great restaurant while you savour his fabulous Chinese dishes. He has backing tapes and sings all the old favourites every night from 9 p.m. til late. The food is wonderful and quite delicious . . . Peking food at its best and with lots of Elvis mementoes around the walls it is a great night out and is often busy so it's advisable to book. If you live in London then you must dine out with Paul Chan at "GRACELANDS PALACE", 881 Old Kent Road, London SE15, tel. 01-639 3961.

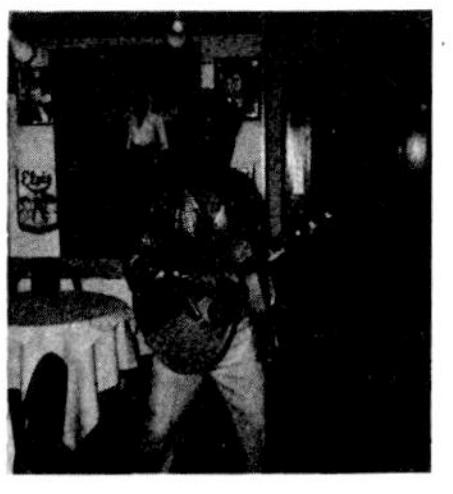

OFFICIAL FIRST DAY COVERS

The most collectible items of memorabilia from the 50th Anniversary Year of ELVIS PRESLEY are the official First Day Covers

Yours Elvisly

DEAR ELVIS

"The day that you left us,
Still stands out clear,
It's hard to imagine
You're no longer here,
You were loved and
respected by, even those
you never met.
An idol like you one just
cannot forget,
How much we miss you,
Just cannot be told,
But you're memory to
me is more precious than gold."

Love Sarah xxx

A BATTLE ROYAL

Can't understand what's going on over there?
This isn't real its got to be a dream,
From the coast of gold across the barren sea,
Graceland's declared war on the likes of you and me!

The "widow" and her lawyer crones are out to
smash us once and for all,
They smear our name and on us pour scorn,
and sadly on our King's memory they care none at all!

But from our battered majestic shores the English
Lion once more does roar!
As Sir Sid leads out in our noble crusade to bury
the evil charges laid.

So take heart my fellow soldiers true,
For we'll triumph of that I am sure!
And once again hold our heads up high,
Towards our beloved King in his heavenly skies.

By Pete Routledge

A STAR ON STAGE

The drum roll first,
To quench our thirst,
The screaming fans' expectations,
And then he came,
A Phoenix from flame,
To a roar of adulation.

A flash of light,
A suit of white,
The hair of sleekest black,
The "legend" was here,
Surrounded by cheers,
Nothing did he lack.

From song to song,
A joke, a smile,
He went through his routine,
Dynamic, Great!
Words could not relate,
The night that we were seeing.

A ballad, some rock,
He watched the clock,
As his love touched us all,
We saw the thing,
A star? A King?
Or just a man who stood so tall.

The last song gone,
Towards the throng,
He knelt with his head bowed,
Then for their cheers,
And loving tears,
He softly thanked the crowd.

The end had come,
And we went home,
To tell our marvellous story,
Held in awe,
We all saw,
The "King" in all his glory.

By Paul Richardson

REMEMBER?

Remember how he started?
Remember how he grew?
Remember how he worked so hard – singing hits for me and you?

Remember how he teased them?
Remember how we'd cry?
Remember that brooding look – then the twinkle in his eye?

Remember how we loved him?
Remember how we'd scream?
Especially when they put him – upon the silver screen?

Not many of us met him – so few got really near,
But none will forget him – of that there is no fear.

He was truly blessed, with talent, good humour, sense of fun,
And love overflowing – enough for everyone,
Remember, yes we always will, for all the things he's done.
And thank the Lord with all our hearts,
For Elvis – the best and only one.

By Pamela Gale from her book of Elvis poems

THE KING

Softness, silence, darkness,
Then a flash of light, a clash of metal,
He appeared,
Draped in white, yet his hair as black as a raven,
He surveyed his subject,
A King of millions.

We stood transfixed by this god,
A roll of thunder and the vision moved,
Chameleon lights darted,
The magic had begun.

He smiled and a long, calm vibrating note echoed
all around.

With immaculate command,
He manipulated the audience,
He was perfection,
He was Elvis, King of Rock and Roll.

By Shona McFarlane

THE AMERICAN DREAM

A poor and humble beginning,
With the fire of ambition inside,
His desire to taste the winning,
But also the wanting to hide.
To fight for what he believed in,
In a way, that was his own,
The path was not always easy,
Uncertainty sometimes was shown.

There were the good and the bad times,
Joy and the sad times too,
But with faith from above, devotion and love,
The charisma and talent shone through.

He scaled the peaks of achievement,
The proof we all have seen,
Forever he will be remembered,
As the Great American Dream.

By Pamela Gale
from "ELVIS IN MY WORDS"

I MET HIM TODAY

I found you in amongst all others,
With scratches and cracks and dog-earred covers,
Your face shone out like a trapped moonbeam,
With eyes all starry, as if in a dream.

After wiping the dust from your heavenly sleeve,
I placed you on the turntable and then, what relief,
Your voice was unhurt and strong as could be,
And say "How Great Thou Art" especially for me.

By Paul Brewer

ELVIS, TAKE MY HAND

When the darkness surrounds me,
Elvis, take my hand.
When I'm afraid and lonely,
Help me to understand.

Stay by my side Elvis,
Help me keep the burning candle
alight.
Show me the path I have to take,
Lead me to all that's right.

Watch over me Elvis,
With all your love and care,
Give me a sign Elvis,
So I know that you are there.

Elvis hear my plea,
Elvis hear my call,
I'm tired and I'm weary,
And I need you most of all.

By Diane Burgess

TO ELVIS

If love could build a staircase,
And memories a lane,
I'd find my way to heaven,
And bring you back again.

By Lisa Gilbert

THE KING IS DEAD

The year was nineteen seventy seven,
August 16th, that fatal day,
On the news at ten it was stated,
that Elvis Presley has passed away,
He'd been found on the floor of his bathroom,
a suspected heart attack it said,
and on arrival at Memphis Baptist hospital,
a doctor had pronounced him dead.

I sat there for several moments
numbness flowing through my brain,
It couldn't be true, I must have misheard,
or misunderstood the name.
Turning on my radio, I searched the dial
for some news to prove me wrong,
then I stopped on a local station
that was playing an Elvis song.

As the song "My Way" drew to a close,
a voice confirmed my fears,
gone was the friend who'd influenced me most
from my early teenage years.
My own teenage daughter came in just then
and asked me what was new?
So I broke the sad news as best I could,
for she worshipped Elvis too.

Well, we got all his records out
that we'd gathered through the years,
and then we played them one by one,
we couldn't hide the tears.
We sat there both of us crying,
that night neither went to bed,
Two generations united in grief,
that the King of Rock was dead.

By Don O'Sullivan

That teenage daughter now has a daughter of her own and her
name? Elvisa, of course.

A CONCERT SO RARE

The lights are dim, the stage is bare,
The music is rising, and he's standing there.
I cannot believe it, I've waited so long,
I hope he will sing my favourite song.

I sit there spellbound, it feels so unreal,
Can he really be up there, can I reach up and feel?
I cannot move; I have to take this all in,
When all of a sudden he smiles with "that" grin.

Was that for me, or someone behind?
He seems so gentle and loving and kind,
He does it again – I'm going out of my mind.
Somebody pinch me – I'm suspended in time.

I find myself standing, and I can't think why,
Clapping and cheering – when I'm really quite shy,
He has this hold, that compels you to stare,
Am I still dreaming, or is he still there?

I came back to my senses – when I fell off my chair,
The floor felt quite hard as I made my way there;
Flat on my back I decided to go,
How it all happened I really don't know.

Elvis bent down looking slightly bemused,
He said "Are you OK or are you confused?"
"Knocked out by your singing," was my reply,
As my eyes tried to focus this vision on high.

His arms went around me, as he lifted me clear,
I gazed at his eyes, was I really this near?
He smiled – then it came – that wonderful kiss,
Of that I can tell you – was absolute bliss.

I wanted to stay, of that I was sure,
I felt almost glad I had hit the floor,
For if this mishap had not taken place,
We would never have ever come face to face.

To continue my story on a more serious line,
A greater singer than Elvis, you never will find.
The king that we know, made me queen for a day,
No one else on this earth can make me feel that way.

His personal gift I always will treasure,
For that moment in time, there will be no measure,
But time marches on in it's own sweet way,
Don't you wish it was you, who fell that day?

By Carole Pitts

Yours Elvisly

PERSONAL TRIBUTES
BY ELVIS FANS

17

HAVE FUN WITH ELVIS

SUPPORTING ACTORS

ACTORS	ROLE	FILM
Charles Bronson		
Richard Egan		
Rudy Vallee		
Bill Bixby		
Alejandro Rey		
Gary Lockwood		
Harry Morgan		
Burgess Meredith		
Walter Matthau		
Regis Toomey		
Mickey Shaughnessy		
Will Hutchins		
Jack Albertson		
Arthur O'Connell		
Michael Ansara		

This quiz will show who knows about Elvis films, how many can you get right? All you have to do is match-up Elvis supporting actor with the film and role the actor played. Good luck, you'll need it!

ROLE	FILM
Cell-mate	KING CREOLE
Water-ski instructor	HARUM SCARUM
Elvis' father	SPEEDWAY
Fight trainer	CHANGE OF HABIT
Racketeer	JAILHOUSE ROCK
Elvis older brother	KISSIN' COUSINS
Evil Prince Dragna	FRANKIE & JOHNNY
Elvis' ''Pop''	CLAMBAKE
Elvis' boss	WORLD'S FAIR
Best friend & manager	FOLLOW THAT DREAM
Father Gibbons	KID GALAHAD
Lifeguard	FUN IN ACAPULCO
Pilot	LOVE ME TENDER
Captain Robert Salbo	SPEEDWAY
Piano player	STAY AWAY, JOE

DID YOU KNOW?

1. Who produced Kid Galahad?

2. What movie company filmed Follow that Dream?

3. Who was Elvis' leading lady in It Happened at The World's Fair?

4. Who wrote the screenplay for Girls, Girls, Girls?

5. Who produced Girl Happy?

6. What role did Elvis play in Easy Come, Easy Go?

7. Who was Elvis' leading lady in Stay Away Joe?

8. Who directed Live a Little, Love a Little?

ELVIS ALBUM ANAGRAM

1. Tron Cince Slive.

2. Plan Caco Fuuin.

3. Dye Mob Lou.

4. Thou Deem Che.

5. Shear Stunye.

6. This Tie Thaws Tay.

7. Lean Nek Value Roll Woy.

8. Vile Show in Dooly.

9. Dove Bery Cymon.

10. Byte Name Did Lou.

DELIBERATE MISTAKES

How many deliberate mistakes can you find in this short Elvis history?
Elvis Jesse Presley was born on August 16th 1935 in the small Alabama town of Tupelo. His parents, Vester and Gladys, worked as share-croppers on the cottonfields and were very poor. As work was scarce in Tupelo, the family moved to Memphis, Tennessee where Elvis attended the County High School. After graduating, Elvis got a job working for the Crown Gas Company as a driver. It was during this time that Elvis made his first record, a Birthday present for his father, at Sam Phillips' Sun Recording Studio.
After hearing about Elvis from his receptionist, Sam invited Elvis back to record a few more numbers with the help of local mucisians Bill Moore and Scotty Black. Elvis was able to re-create the sound of the black blues singers together with a hillbilly beat and the results were sensational. The records Sam released did well locally, and it soon became clear Sun Records just couldn't cope with National demand. Phillips sold Elvis' contract to Columbia Records for $35,000 but a change of heart by the executives there gave RCA the chance to sign Elvis up themselves. And so Elvis became RCA's biggest recording star with number one after number one on both sides of the Atlantic. Elvis' fame spread world-wide and the hits just kept on coming. Movies were next, and Elvis made the trip to Hollywood for his first film ''Loving You''. The fans flocked to see Elvis on screen and he also became one of Americas most popular movie stars.
Elvis, just like any other American man, was drafted in 1959. He joined-up with the U.S. Marines and was stationed in France. It was here that Elvis met his future wife, Priscilla, the daughter of his commanding officer. After his national service was over, Elvis moved-in to his new home in Memphis called 'Graceland'. His career was unaffected by his years in the forces and a film of his adventures was quickly made. Throughout the sixties, Elvis continued to record great records and starred in many films, including ''Roustaround'', ''It Happened At The Worlds Fair'', ''Spinoff'', ''Blue Hawaii'', ''Paradise Hawaiian Style'' and ''A Stone For Danny Fisher''. But Elvis had not performed before his fans for many years, so in 1969 he was persuaded to make a T.V. Special for the ABC network. The show was a tremendous success and this encouraged Elvis to play a season of dates in the Las Vegas area. He later went on tour and performed another T.V. special in Hawaii during 1974. Other countries visited by Elvis included Canada, Scotland, West Germany and Japan, although British fans were sadly never to see him appear on stage.
The tragic news of his passing came on a sad January night in 1977. Elvis, in body, was dead, but his spirit and legend will live on forever.

WORD SEARCH
Streets Elvis Lived On

```
C A D A D N I L E C A L P A C C O R
A Y O L L I H H E L P G F E L D C B
N A T L K J I L H I O I G O L E B E
T W T U T S A R I N P Q P O E N M I
W A I A Z D Y X L D L W V N W J N T
E I E G S F E D L A A C O B T A O T
L G K U J A M I E J R Y I H E M Y O
L U O W A S H I N G T O N L G I N D
S R T A M M Y R Q F P O N O M E A N
T E D A V I S Z I Y X W O V U T C O
I P H U G O F F E A D D C B E A O R
T S D R Q P Y O N L M M L A L J R N
W U V S M A D A I A U R A M A L I H
A C B A W N Z Y N B H O R N V X H G
K J I H E H G F E A L A K E O D C R
O N G E Y M M A T M M I S S N M L E
T I R S R Q P D R A V E L U O B P E
H G A Z Y N O B U D U A X W M V U N
```

Look for the names of the streets that Elvis lived on. From Memphis to Los Angeles to Mississippi, these streets, roads, boulevards, and highways should be familiar to Elvis fans. Circle the words listed below and you'll find out the names of many of the streets. Solution to this puzzle will appear in the next issue of The Record.

Adams	E.P. Boulevard	Lamar	Perugia Way
Alabama	Getwell	Monovale	Poplar
Audubon	Goodman	North Green	Rocca Place
Belogio			Trousdale
Chino Canyon	Highway Fifty One		Washington

TRUE OR FALSE

1. Billy Smith is Elvis' cousin.

2. Elvis used to smoke cigars.

3. Elvis didn't like motorcycles.

4. Elvis used to take piano lessons.

5. Elvis' biggest selling album was. How Great Thou Art.

6. Elvis usually paid around $50,000 for his jump suits.

7. One of Elvis' favourite recordings was Unchained Melody.

8. Elvis' favourite breed of dog was Chow-Chow.

9. Elvis' favourite colour was yellow.

10. Charlie Hodge, Elvis' friend first met him at Humes High School.

WORD SEARCH
ELVIS' CHRISTMAS SONGS

```
L K C A B Y B A B Y M G N I R B A T N A S A
O I I E A U O Y E V O L I L R A T Y L L C E
U B T C D F G H J K L M N P Q R S T V W X Y
N W O T N I K C A B S I S U A L C A T N A S
E A N M L L D C B S U V X R T U O I E A Z I
I W H I T E C H R I S T M A S O U T R S A L
X R Q Z A U T E R C E S O N S I T I O I E E
S T U L A D D O O G M I K E Y B A F N O D N
N A A N E T Y D W U J Y D N A E R A S I L T
T B S O K A E Z E N N Y A W E L I F F U B N
I L L B E H O M E F O R C H R I S T M A S I
N U Y A W E I F F U B F O S D E N A T I G G
E E N A E E E N R E N Y B A W V Y M M A T H
D C N A A N E T E N Y A W E A E Y R R E J T
A H M I K Y D U J Y D N A R T N A E N Y A W
D R O L S U O I C E R P D N A H Y M E K A T
N I O D P E A C E I N T H E V A L L E Y P N
A S M I K A E S I L M I K E Y A F E A N O D
L T W D M C B O I E A C B A A S I L H Y A S
A M G I E A L Y A L L E N Y A W Y R R E J T
L A R O F R L A L D M C R A G E E N E R M L
O S A S U A L C A T N A S S E M O C E R E H
```

Christmas was one of Elvis' favorite times of the year. His Christmas songs are a poignant reminder of him this time of the year. Circle the names of Elvis' Christmas songs below.

Blue Christmas	Peace In The Valley
Here Comes Santa Claus	Santa Claus is Back in Town
I Believe	Santa Bring My Baby Back
I'll Be Home For Christmas	Silent Night
It Is No Secret	Take My Hand Precious Lord
(Oh) Little Town of Bethlehem	White Christmas

FLIP SIDES. . .
Match the 'B' Sides with each of the 'A' Sides for the singles above.

'B' SIDES	
A	Lawdy Miss Clawdy
B	Don't Be Cruel
C	Tutti Frutti
D	Loving Your
E	Thats When The Heartaches Begin
F	A Mess Of Blues
G	Treat Me Nice
H	Any Way You Want Me
I	My Wish Come True
J	Play For Keeps

'A' SIDES	
1	Jail House Rock
2	Blue Suede Shoes
3	All Shook Up
4	A Big Hunk O'Love
5	Too Much
6	Shake Rattle & Roll
7	Hound Dog
8	Teddy Bear
9	Love Me Tender
10	Its Now Or Never

ELVIS FILM ANAGRAMS

1	Bleet Out His Rith Wirl
2	Urah Sham Cur
3	Twist This At Heary
4	A Gassy Eye Coome
5	Came Balk
6	Oh La Let Down Frami
7	Whalie Abui
8	A Wet Jay Soya
9	So Put In
10	Phar Pigy

THE ELVISLY YOURS CENTRE

The Elvisly Yours Centre was officially opened on January 9th, 1983 by Jerry and Myrna Schilling.

Original film poster from Charro adjacent to 11½ ft. high photo of Elvis.

The all Elvis jukebox flanked by an 8ft. high photo of Elvis.

Jerry and Myrna and Sid toast the new Elvisly Yours Centre.

Sid Shaw (founder of Elvisly Yours) and Elvis.

The beautiful birthday cake baked by Ann Medhurst which was presented to St. Marys Hospital Paddington (where Prince William was born)—a hospital fit for a KING.

The Elvisly Yours Centre is open every day Monday-Saturday 10am-6pm (Saturday closes 4pm) and on Sunday 10am-4pm July, August and December until Xmas. Every January 8th and August 16th we host an Elvis FREE CONVENTION at the Centre. All fans welcome from all over the world.

**ELVISLY YOURS CENTRE
107 SHOREDITCH HIGH ST. LONDON E1 6JN
Tel: 071-739 2001 Fax: 071-739 2002**

LETTERS LETTERS LETTERS LETTERS

Dear Sir,
After a lot of struggling, I am at last applying to your "Elvisly Yours'. God knows why, I've only been an El fan for two years, so I don't even have nostalgia as an excuse!! I've got everything I need for a happy life, and it is, so why do I love Elvis? I've read all the bad things, and the good things, got a great collection of 'his' fabulous music, and decided the credits outweight the debits by far. Saw your piece in "The Daily Mirror", wrote for a mag. and here I am. Looking forward to next August, please try to keep going, you're a great comfort. People like you are the answer to what Elvis was always looking for. I hope he knows. Dear Sid, dear fans, dear Elvis.
Babs Bradley, Berkshire

Dear Mr Shaw,
On behalf of the London Hospital I would like to thank you for the beautiful cake you donated on 9 January.
One of our staff retired after 37 years service and we felt it would be appropriate to use the cake as the centrepiece of his retirement party. It was both admired and enjoyed by everyone.
We will send a photograph in due course.
Thank you again for your generosity.
Yours sincerely Anne Anderson
Outpatient Services Manager
The London Hospital
Whitechapel

Dear Sid,
Sorry no cards this year, but I sent my money to the Trauma Unit, Baptist Hospital, Memphis. Thought it made more sense.
Well Sid, its been quite a year hasn't it? May I say thank you sincerely for TCE and for uniting countries and bringing people together like with Koyla Vasin etc and its fans throughout the world stood up shoulder to shoulder — we could move mountains!! You know Sid it's love that makes the world go round, it's the sharing and the caring — it's not the almighty dollar — Elvis knew it and we shouldn't forget it — let's hope and pray 1990 will be a loving and happy year all past disputes forgotten — if the Berlin Wall can come tumbling down — maybe prejudice can too. Let's hope so, because Elvis' family of friends, all of us, DO CARE.
May I wish you and yours a very happy Christmas time and all the best for the coming new year 1990. I hope you will carry on TCE for many many years to come. He gave us so much of himself.
God bless and take care, please spare a prayer for Elvis' grandchild and his daughter. I honestly believe they are in need of one! A pity they don't have the Smith and Presley families behind them!! (family values etc). Pris calls them all Hillbillies!! Nuf said!!.
All my best etc.
Sally Foster
Victoria, Australia

Dear Mr Shaw,
Thank you for coming to speak to our class. We have learned a great deal about our country and people. Most of all we have learned to appreciate happenings in our city we take for granted. I don't think Memphians really know how Elvisly Yours and fans from around the world help the city's economy. I guess people overlook things which they grew up with.
Thanks again for your visit; it was very interesting for the students.
Sincerely yours,
Tom Brittain and Economics Classes
Southern Baptist Educational Center,
Memphis Tennessee

Dear Sid,
Our experience on October 20, 1986 was, indeed, one to always be remembered. Your creative idea of bringing handicapped persons to Memphis as a part of your "Elvisly Yours" tour is fantastic. Your hard work to make it a reality is honorable. As you suggested, "let's make it an annual event".
Enclosed are the set of colored pictures recording this historic occasion. Also, included is my article describing the event.
Please let us know how the final episode of this saga is received on "Surprise! Surprise!".
Thank you for delivering our packets to John Oliver and the staff at London Weekend Television. It was our pleasure to meet and work with you.
Sincerely
Ann H. Welch, Assistant Director,
Division of Special Education, Memphis City Schools
Memphis Tennessee

Dear Sid,
I hope you will accept my poem I have tried to write about Priscilla and the Graceland lawyers. I know that you are a 100% Elvis Presley fan despite what Todd Slaughter says, because of the way your fan club has built up bigger, every year. I have just started work again so I hope that I would be able to run a fan club branch as well, I was also wondering if you know when the date is, when the Elvis exhibition comes to Edinburgh, I have looked through all the free newspapers here, but have never seen it yet, and I don't want to miss it, I had to miss Alan Bleasdale's "are you lonesome tonight" because of work, I work late, I have also been to a couple of Elvis Conventions in Edinburgh which were good and I went to the Forever Elvis play which I thought was okay. I like Jim White, but he could never be liked as much as Elvis, well, here's hoping you'll like my poems (on the other side).
Goodbye for now, Peter Lyons
Midlothian, Scotland

Graceland house, was full of love,
before the King departed,
but now, Priscilla, in a huff,
She went and turned, coldhearted.

She took the fan club to the court,
to try and beat the law,
but we won't let that, ever happen,
as we've got Sid Shaw.

He hopes to win it, so do we, to stop her,
being so cruel,
I wished that she would leave us be,
and stop this, playing the fool.

But Sid will win it, this I know,
because he's got it right,
and if she wants to keep on trying,
then we will, really fight.

P.S. Priscilla, Priscilla, with your money,
you could buy a palace,
As I know, it's all from Elvis, why are you
in Dallas?

Hello Sid,
Just a few lines to say thanks for holiday Oct. 1988, it was great.
Meeting true Elvis fans and with friends I have made, my life has changed, I thank you all.
So I will be seeing your Oct 1989.
I would like to wish you a happy and peaceful New Year and thank you again.
From Jukebox Reg
Skegness
A proud member of the Elvisly Yours Fan Club and one of the "Four White Virgins", Memphis '88.

Dear Mr Shaw,
Thank you very much for your thoughtfulness in sending me the beautiful colour photograph of the Elvis statue standing in our foyer, together with two issues of ELVIS. I was very pleased to see the excellent spread you gave to Capital in the magazine.
I am passing on your useful information about Charlie Hodge to our Programme Department for their information.
John Whitney
Managing Director
Capital Radio, Euston Tower

Dear Sid,
I hope you won't mind a long story about why Elvis means so much to me.
I am 66 years old (widow), my handicapped son David is 34 years and my daughter is 24 years old.
It is difficult for a mother and her handicapped son (I.Q.68) to find much in common and David has lived in a home owned by the Home Farm Trust, Bristol since he was 20 years old. His appearance is 'normal' but unfortunately he cannot write, and although he can read reasonably well he still couldn't tell you the date of Christmas Day.
David has loved and admired Elvis for fifteen years. I have never really liked pop music, but five years ago I almost by accident heard Elvis sing "Danny Boy" on my radio while doing the ironing in my kitchen.
I was absolutely stunned by the sound of this great voice in my kitchen. Since then I have read and listened to everything about Elvis.
David and I now always have something to talk about, exchange newspaper cuttings about Elvis, and we never have to wonder about Christmas presents.
He gives me soap, and I give him Elvis mugs! I love and admire Elvis something like a son, but more because he has given David a reason for living, and something to talk about on equal terms with anybody. I bet David knows the date of birth of Elvis Presley.
Of course, all my friends and relations think that I am quite mad. All I can say is long live the King — you've done more for us than all our friends and relations put together.
We went to Memphis with Elvisly Yours in October 1984 and it was an unforgettable holiday, with all the friendly (and very tolerant) fans, and meeting such kind and hospitable American people. I remember very well a barbeque — or "cook out", at a very kind person's home, just for us the fans. Two kind people in fact. There was a lovely tree growing in their garden, we had hamburgers and orange juice, and we'll never forget it.We hope to go to Memphis again soon with Elvisly Yours. It's the only holiday I've ever taken without worrying about my age or my son's I.Q.!
Thank You, Yours sincerely
Barbara Smith

Dear Sir,
On 9th January 1982, your organisation kindly donated two large cakes to this hospital, following celebrations for the late Elvis Presley. As these cakes were so generous in size I was able to send some to the Geriatric Wards, the Younger Disabled Unit and the Childrens Ward.
On behalf of the hospital, therefore, I would like to thank you for your gift which was greatly appreciated.
With best wishes.
Yours faithfully
B. D. Aird, Sector Administrator
Leicester General Hospital
Gwendolen Road

Dear Sid,
I have listened to the recent recording of "Spelling on the Stone", which is supposed to be Elvis, well I can honestly say, I have never heard such a load of rubbish in all my life, this person does not even begin to sound like Elvis did, I'd like to know when all of these stories about Elvis being alive is going to stop, what has happened to "respect for the dead", because these people certainly do not know the meaning of it. I don't believe Elvis has faked his own death. I have watched his funeral many times on video, and there is just no way he would have done a cruel thing like that to his fans, let alone his family. Why can't people just let Elvis the King rest in peace and let us the fans remember him the way he was. Elvis I still Love You Tender.
Sincerely yours
Carol Beckham, Newmarket — An upset fan

Dear Mr Shaw,
Ten months ago I watched "That's The Way It Is" on television. At the end I found myself extremely moved. The next day I bought my first record, the LP of Elvis' last performance. After listening to it I was so upset I could not even go out and keep an appointment.
I was frightened and confused by the depths of my emotion, and joined Elvisly Yours to see if any one else had experienced this. To my amazement there was a letter describing my exact feelings. Since then I have pen friends, and with their help, after many months of fighting it, and thinking I was going senile, I have now accepted that Elvis is part of my life. The more I read and watch him I feel there is something spiritual that at times seems to transmit from him. It is not superficial.
Although a widow for nine years, I have good children and friends, but of course get lonely at times. Elvis has helped.
I know you have read letters like this many times, but my point in writing is that I am nearly 65 years old, and I wonder if there is anyone near my age, who has had this experience, so late in life, and the first time ever?
Yours sincerely, Mrs Betty Cole, London N1

Dear Sid,
I wanted to write to you to tell you how much I enjoyed your interview in the "Clothes Show" magazine this month.
Thank you, as always for standing up for Elvis and always being so positive about him. You do so much good in his name. I'm really proud of you and do so hope you will win the battle against the estate. I very much disagree with how the estate runs things. When will they ever get it right?
Another reason for writing was because yesterday I read a brilliant article/open letter about you and the estate (I don't know if you're aware of the article) it was sent with my "Suspicious Minds" fan club newsletter. It was written by an American fan called Sherry Daniel and she was very supportive about you. As I said, you've done so much for Elvis, so many good things. He'd be so honoured and proud of you, as his fans are.
It must be a very tough time for you right now. You're a genuine person and a genuine fan and I wish you all the best with your court battle.
Once again many thanks for all the good you do, you deserve much success.
Take care, fondest regards, God bless you.
Love Jeanette Knight, Norwich, Norfolk

Dear Sid,
I just received a copy of Sherry Daniels letter from Los Angeles, California, Rose Maria Farro Fan Club — North Jersey Knights for Elvis sent it to me and many others.
I was really mad and hurt that Graceland is giving you such a hard time concerning Your Elvis Fan Club.
It seems every time somebody wants to do something nice concerning Elvis, Graceland steps in and wants to stop it because they are not receiving any money out of it.
Beside who is Graceland to tell me what Fan Club I can or cannot join or buy from. As far as I am concerned you can send me an application right now to join your Fan Club.
I am behind you all the way. We Elvis fans have to stick together always.
Yours sincerely, Harold & Myrna Blanck
620 Forman Avenue, Point Pleasant Bch. N.J. 08742

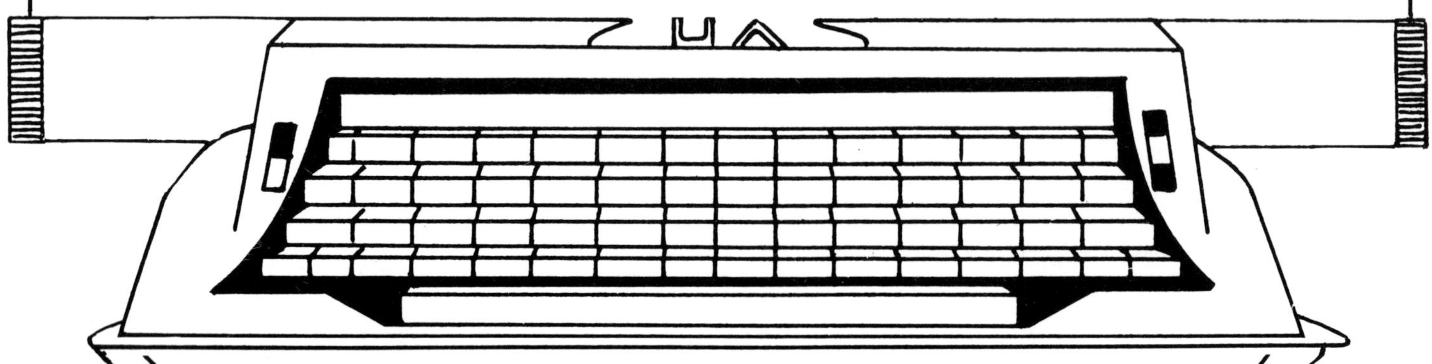

LETTERS TO: "ELVISLY YOURS", P.O. BOX 315, LONDON NW10

LETTERS LETTERS LETTERS LETTERS

Dear Sid,
WORCESTERSHIRE CENTRE CARAVAN CLUB — NEIL WILLIAMS — ELVISLY YOURS FAN CLUB MEMBER.
We would like to thank you so very much for taking the time to send Neil the gifts which were given to him at the time of the "Gracelend" presentation.
As you can imagine he was over the moon with everything. Neil has a lot of memorabilia, but he did not have "Elvis in Quotes" or the '89 calendar. It really was most thoughtful of you. October just cannot come quickly enough for him, and we are now on a countdown. The caravan club responded superbly to him and they can see the excitement build. His life totally revolves around Elvis and I know it will be a real memory for him.
I must say that I (his mum) am getting a bit anxious as I have never been out of the country before, but I hope I can rely on the Elvisly Yours fan club to reassure me.
Our sincere thanks to you once again Sid.
Here's to October "Memphis '89"
Yours sincerely,
Carol & Mel Williams
53 Lynbrook Close, Netherton, Dudley

Dear Sir/Madam,
Please find enclosed £11.00 in cash. I cannot send a cheque as my father hates Elvis and I don't want him to write the cheque out for Elvisly Yours. I am in a rush to catch the post so I will chance sending cash. I am using a friend's address so my Dad wont go mad if he were to see the parcel. Please send as soon as possible as my friend will be going on holiday.
Thanking you,
Your friend,
David Grigsby, Cardiff

The letter to the Sun Newspaper was:

Dear Sir,
I am writing to you to say what a low down, good for nothing, stinking newspaper you run.
I was disgusted to read in your newspaper on the 10th of April this week on page nine, under the title ODDBALLS and subtitle TELLY SHOTS, what you had printed about the late Elvis Presley. For starters your paper said that he was *drug soaked*, what a load of old rubbish, if your paper had ever bothered to read the autopsey report, you would have found out that the drugs found on him were for his nervous and overweight problems, just in order to prove this I have listed the ten drugs listed in the autopsey report, and all ten were *within* the THERAPUTIC LEVELS, and were prescribed by his doctor.
HYCODAN — a cough tablet, CODEINE — a pain killer, DEMEROL — a sedative and pain killer, VALIUM — a tranquilliser and muscle relaxant, CORTISONE — a pain killer used against the lupus disease, VALMID — a sedative and hypnotic QUAALUDE — a sedative, often used as a sleeping pill, BABITUATES — Depressants which work on the central nervous system, DILAUDID — a sedative and pain killer, PERCODAN — A sedative and pain killer.
Also you had put in your article that Elvis kept a *sub-machine gun* with him whenever he watched television, rubbish, he kept a small revolver with him. Also you said "If a particular programme displeased him, he would lose his temper and let fly at the screen in a hail of bullets", again rubbish the only time Elvis shot at the television, was when something about him came on, and even if he did shoot his T.V. set its got naff-all to do with the press, expecially six coming on seven years after his death.
And why is it I very rarely read about people like John Lennon who took drugs just so they could get high, it seems the only time you print anything about ROCK STARS be them dead or alive, its always a load of nonesense.
From what I can read you're newspaper shows no respect for the dead, I've no doubt that there are many Elvis fans around the country who are angered and upset about what rubbish was written.
And the last thing is isn't it about time your newspaper let Elvis rest in peace instead of writing about him whenever you get the chance.
Yours faithfully S. Marshall ,Basildon, Essex.

Dear Sid,
I'd just like to say a big Thank You for the super day you gave us on Elvis' birthday, I and my friends enjoyed ourselves tremendously. It was great being able to listen to Jerry and his wife, not forgetting David Hamilton who was terrific. I look forward to the next event which you may decide to organise in the near future.
I have a suggestion for your magazine. I think it would be a good idea to have a section for penfriends or certain ads concerning fans who wish to swap or sell items on Elvis. I think it would be great for your magazine, what do you think Sid?
Let me know, I enclose a 15½p stamp for your convenience. Keep on Rockin.
To the greatest fella there ever was,
Elvisly,
Eva Borthiewicz, Banbury, Oxon.

Dear Elvisly Yours,
I felt I just had to write and thank you for printing my name in the latest edition of Elvisly Yours at the "pen pals" section. As a result I now have over 10 pen-pals and the letters are still coming! It's wonderful to be able to write to someone who loves Elvis. Before, I didn't know any Elvis fans. In the past, I've written to various magazines and nothing's ever happened, so you can imagine how I felt when I saw my name in your magazine.
Let me just say that your magazine is a fantastic read, always with exciting and interesting news. As far as other Elvis magazines that I've bought go, Elvisly Yours really is in a class of its own. You almost feel part of a family when you read it.
The choice of records, books and memorabilia is amazing. I've been buying Elvisly Yours since August, but this is the first time I've been able to afford anything from it. (Even now, the bill comes to just £2.25!) I would buy the whole magazine out if I could, I'd really like to make out a subscription for Elvisly Yours as I don't want to risk missing any, but my money just has to go on "other things" my mum tells me.
I know after all you've done for me that I'd be pushing my luck to expect a reply to this letter, but I've enclosed an SAE just in case.
Keep up the good work! I wish you luck in the next round of your battle"!
Elvisly Yours
Glenda

Dear Sir,
After buying my first "Elvisly Yours" magazine and reading it I thought I'd write to your letters section and tell you how much I enjoyed it. I was wondering how often the Elvisy Yours magazine comes out as I have No. 26 and haven't seen any more since.
The main reason I'm writing this letter is to let all you English Elvis fans know that there are quite a few Aussie fans around also (as so all over the world). Although I'm only 14 I absolutely idolise "Elvis Presley". Everyday I wish to myself that I could have been born a lot earlier than I was. I don't have much interest in seeing America, but my biggest wish in the world is to visit Graceland, to me it would be as good as going to heaven and personally meeting him. Not many of my wishes come true but one day, somehow, I'll get there. I know most of you fans reading this are probably saying "it's our wish too", well I have one thing to say, "if you believe in your wish it will one day come true even if it doesn't seem possible" — keep saving!!!
Yours sincerely
Clare Byrne
Perth, Australia

Dear Sid and all at Elvisly Yours,
Firstly to you Sid, may I say congratulations! I was very very proud of you as you stood up on the platform during the by-election. I stayed up till the declaration and for a golden oldie that doesn't often happen. I had a lot of tape in the video and each time you got a long shot of the candidates there was our beloved Elvis clearer than anyone else. Thanks Sid you are great and "not bad looking either".
There seems to be a thousand things I want to say but the words won't come. How I wish I was able to travel down to your events. I had a lot of great reports about Larry's visit. Diana and Ray are good friends of mine so I heard a lot from them but also from penfriends who were there, a great time was had by all no mistake.
I'm dying to know if you are any further on with the plans to have one of the events in Scotland, all we have meantime is the annual Scottish Convention in Edinburgh. That's a dream day for us Elvis starved fans up here and more especially the older ones who can't travel very far. (I get around on two sticks most of the time). I'm sure that there would be a good turn out for you up in the frozen north and I sure would be there as well as my best friend Rita Watt from Aberdeen.
Talking about Aberdeen. We still haven't heard anything from Tom who had a letter in your last issue about starting something in Aberdeen. I'm in contact with a number of teenagers who desperately want and need something so I've advised them to write to you.
Sorry folks but my brain has gone into reverse gear. Just can't get the motor runnin' at all. Some sort of fuel starvation I guess. Oh while I remember I was lying in bed one morning when the following verse came into my mind and wouldn't go away till I wrote it down, see what you think _

A MESSAGE

Last night I dreamed of Elvis,
He says he's doin' fine!
He says he's very busy,
And not for us to pine,
The hours are long but happy,
There is no day or night,
But love is wide and endless,
Like a warm blinding light.
He knows how much we love him,
And he's very pleased to say,
The love he sends right back to us
Brings us closer day by day.
Elvis loves us all so deeply,
No earthly love compare,
He watches carefully over us
And hopes we are aware,
He's still taking care of business
And we must do the same
He says unite and conquer
Divided we're fair game!!!

I'm not sure why I had to write it down but it seems to be in what Larry Geller had to say.
I'll let you be the judge anyway.
Take care, God Bless,Elvisly always,
Netta McHardy
Kincardineshire, Scotland.

Dear Fans,
We would like to thank you for making our visit to London to celebrate Elvis' birthday a very memorable one.
The fans here really and truly love Elvis, we could feel that, and we also felt that love through the genuine hospitality that you gave to us. Elvis' memory will remain alive through the love and dedication of his friends; he would have loved to have called you his friends.
Until we meet again,
We wish you love,
Myrna and Jerry Schilling

Dear Sid,
Thank you for your letter concerning your recent visit to Memphis. I was delighted to have the opportunity to talk with you and I was overwhelmed by your generosity in presenting me with the momentoes of Elvis. I was proud to have been considered a friend of his and enjoyed reminiscing on those early years with you and your friends.
In addition, I appreciate your efforts to keep alive the true spirit and meaning of Elvis' life. You have the gratitude of his millions of fans who continue to pay tribute to his extraordinary life, talent, and determination. When possible, I will attempt to draft a brief history of my connection with Elvis and search my files for unreleased photographs.
Again, thank you for the letter, but most importantly, thank you for dropping by my office for a visit. Whenever I can be of help to you, please feel free to call on me.
Sincerely yours
William M. Morris, Jr.
Shelby County Mayor

Dear Mr Shaw,
I feel I must write and thank you for the latest issue of Elvisly Yours, it was well worth waiting for. The free poster is simply marvellous, a truly beautiful picture of Elvis. I do congratulate you on a wonderful magazine, with the lovely photos and all the Elvis souvenirs and magazines it must be the best one ever. You are doing a wonderful job in keeping the memory of Elvis alive. I have been very pleased with all the souvenirs and magazines I've had. I have quite a collection of books, large and small, and spend many happy hours looking through them. With my many cassettes I can and do lose myself in a world of Elvis, he was a great and wonderful man. Thanks again for all you are doing and the lovely magazine.
Mrs E. Pratt, Norwich

Dear Elvisly Yours
My friend and I are both 15, and for a GCSE English project, we were recently assigned to write an advert for an imaginary product of our choice.
My friend and I invented Presley's peanut butter. The advert had to be made for a radio station, so there were no visual effects.
We thought you might like to see it, and thanks to Elvis' singing we got a good grade for once!!
The black writing is one of us speaking, and the italic is Elvis replying.

PRESLEY'S PEANUT BUTTER

Are you fed up of the same old spread?
Are you ready for something new?
Elvis: I'm a ready, ready, ready
(From Ready Teddy)
Do you want to know what you're really eating?
Elvis: I gotta know, gotta know, gotta know
(Gotta know)
Then Presley's peanut butter is what you're looking for. The most unique, original, incredible crunchy taste ever invented!
Elvis: That's a matter of fact buddy, and you know it well
(U.S. male)
It tastes so good it even makes Elvis go!
Elvis: Mmmm
(Don't be cruel)
So spread the word of this great new spread
Elvis: I'm gonna tell my moma and my papa too
(I'm gonna sit right down and cry)
15 per cent proceeds go to charity, so by feeding yourself you'll be feeding millions of starving children
Elvis: Well, the world turns . . .
(2nd verse of In the ghetto)
Try it and keep the legend alive!
Elvis: (Laughter . . . fading away)
(Are you lonesome tonight)
Keep Rockin
Fiona Gilmore

Well done Fiona and friend — great advert!

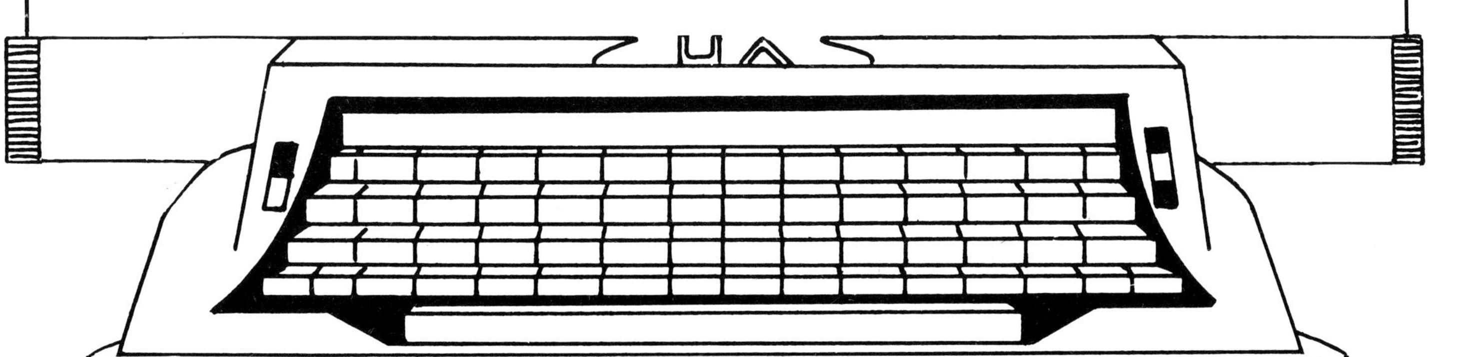

LETTERS TO: "ELVISLY YOURS", P.O. BOX 315, LONDON NW10

THE ELVIS PRESLEY ESTATE ACCOUNTS (Extracts)

After months of painstaking research we are proud to bring to Elvis Fans throughout the world extracts from the account of the Estate of Elvis Presley. To date accounts of Elvis Presley Enterprises and Graceland are not available since the Trustees run Graceland as a private company. However this glimpse into where the money comes from and goes is enlightening.

From an early issue of Elvisly Yours before the Probate Court lost its power in 1985.

1984

(year ending July 31st)

INCOME

Total	$1,844,043.17
Some items of revenue	
RCA instalment	$111,000.00
Chappell & Co	$1,056,668.40
Transfer from Account	
No 500196 Colonel Parker	$15.89
Miscellaneous Royalties	$69,425.90
William Morris Agency	$69,149.91
Interest on George Nich Polous Note	$14,306.23

EXPENDITURE

Total	$1,351,306.07
Some Expenses	
Fee for Singer Out Take	$23,333.33
Payments to Priscilla B Presley for Lisa Marie Presley	
Tuitioning	$960.00
Child Support	$48,000.00
Half food and house help	$14,700.00
Mrs P. Presley Travel	$2,262.00
Executors Fee	$255,000.00
(trustees Priscilla, Hanks and NBC)	
Joseph Rascoff and Co	$78,000.00
Glankler Brown etc Law Firm	$41,115.76
Insurance Premium for Lisa Presley	$314.50
Federal Judiciary Taxes	$525,000.00
Little Page and Webner (Law Firm)	$43,240.16
Hanks Partin and Garrett	$10,281.28
Accounts	
User Fee to RCA Don't be Cruel	$62,500.00
Parcher and Herbert (Law Firm)	$3C,895.92
Some Security Transactions	
Acquired rights per settlement with RCA	1,000,000.00
Delivered to Joan Deary	
Six various tapes of ELVIS MUSIC	$1.00
STUTZ BLACKHAWK Charged off and delivered to Trust	$1.00
Jewelery charged off and delivered to Trust	$4,435.00

Balance of Hand as of 31st July 1984	$6,639,346.59

1983

INCOME

Total	$1,815,986.46
Some items of income	
Box Car Enterprises	$27,061.97
RCA	$378,236.54
Donations at Graceland	$373.50
Miscellaneous Royalties	$73,247.46
William Morris Agency	$71,501.18
Damilo Printing Co	$15,573.09
Home Box Office	$22,00.00
U.S. Treasury Tax Refund	$93,017.45

EXPENDITURE

Total	$1,755,571.28
Some Expenses	
Federal Judiciary Tax	$150,000.00
Federal Estate Tax Instalment	$108,591.36
Payments to Priscilla for Lisa	
Tutioning	$6,240.00
Educational Reinbursements	$5,145.00
Child Support	$48,000.00
Half Salary and Food Expenses	$13,800.00
Lisa Marie Travel	$868.12
Mrs P. Presley Travel	$2,008.00
Executors Fee	
(Trustees)	$90,000.00
Box Car	$100,000.00
Parcher and Herbert (Lawyers)	$81,579.35
Roger Toll (lawyer)	$37,105.21
Parcher and Herbert	$74,866.78
Robert and Holland Lawyers	$42,858.97
Glankler Brown etc (lawyers)	$184,647.57
Glankler Brown etc	$44,730.00
Hanks Partin and Garrett	$12,990.00
(accountants)	$13,048.51
D. Beecher Smith (lawyer)	$18,374.19

1982

(year ending July 31st)

INCOME

Total	$2,464,955.80
Some items of income	
RCA	$538,041.64
Chappell and Co	$714,008.83
Royalties from Box Car	$141,161.33
Motion Pictures	
Allied Artists	$23,333.36
MGM	$51,574.79
United Artists	$99,132.04
Viacom	$12,524.16
Songwriter Royalties	
Chappell	$39.753.77
Fan Donations	$688.79
Interest	$425,683.75
Withheld from Colonel Parker by Court	$679,157.29

EXPENDITURE

Total	$2,022,705.22
Executors Fees	$210,000.00
Legal and Acounting	$812,273.65
Salaries and Wages	$132,387.00
Security Service	$171,179.55
Federal Income Tax	$458,855.00
Telephone	$4,315.43
Utilities	$20,109.29
Advertising and Publicity	$3,120.56
Maintenance, Repairs, Storage	$29,598.22
Alimony and Child Support	$48,000.00

OTHER INTERESTING FACTS FROM THE ACCOUNTS

Colonel Parker

From Elvis death to May 1980 the approximate funds paid to Parker were $4.3 million from Elvis' earnings (only approximate and for managing a man who was dead).

Rascoff

For all services rendered $12,000.00 per month ($144,000.00 year) and Rascoff **does not** have to devote his entire time attention and energies to the business of Presley and may engage in the business activities of other artists. Not bad over £100,000 per year for a part time job.

Assets at 31st July 1981

Grand Total	**$8,489,798.71**
Some Examples of Assets	
Graceland (value)	561,165.58
Trophy Room Equipment:	
Furniture	13,925.00
Trophies	29,300.00
Jewelry	4,435.00
Auto & Trucks	100,213.37
Horses	2,100.00
Household Furnishings & Clothing	216,265.00
Musical Equipment	3,475.00
Copyright Royalty Rights (Chappel & Co)	1,352,063.43
TV Specials	225,000.00
Government Bonds	1,736,146.00

These figures are MIND BOGLING and are only partial accounts. All the millions going through Graceland are not available and the many licensing deals are all hidden in the accounts of Elvis Presley Enterprises.

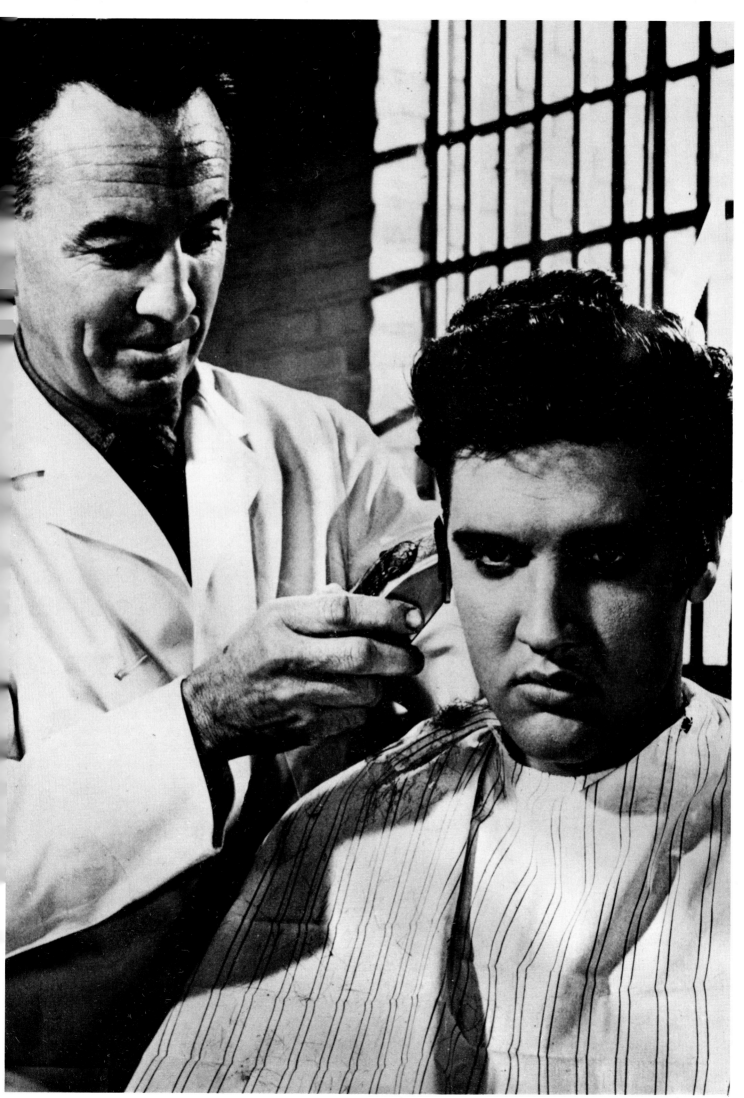

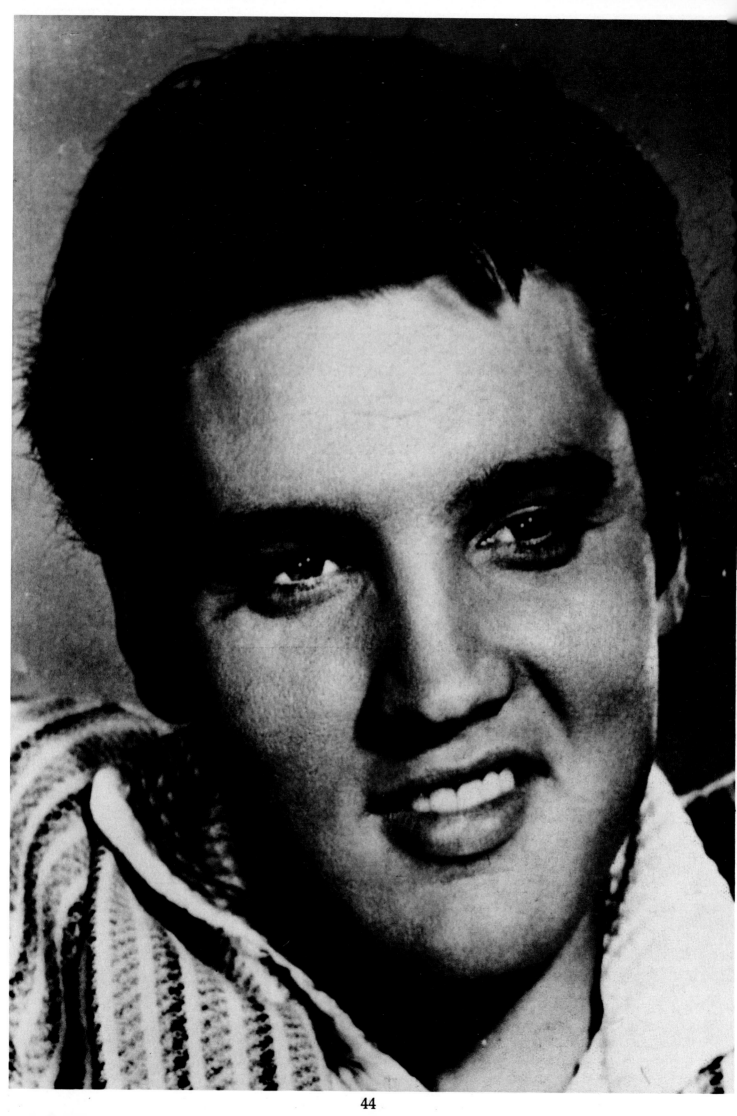

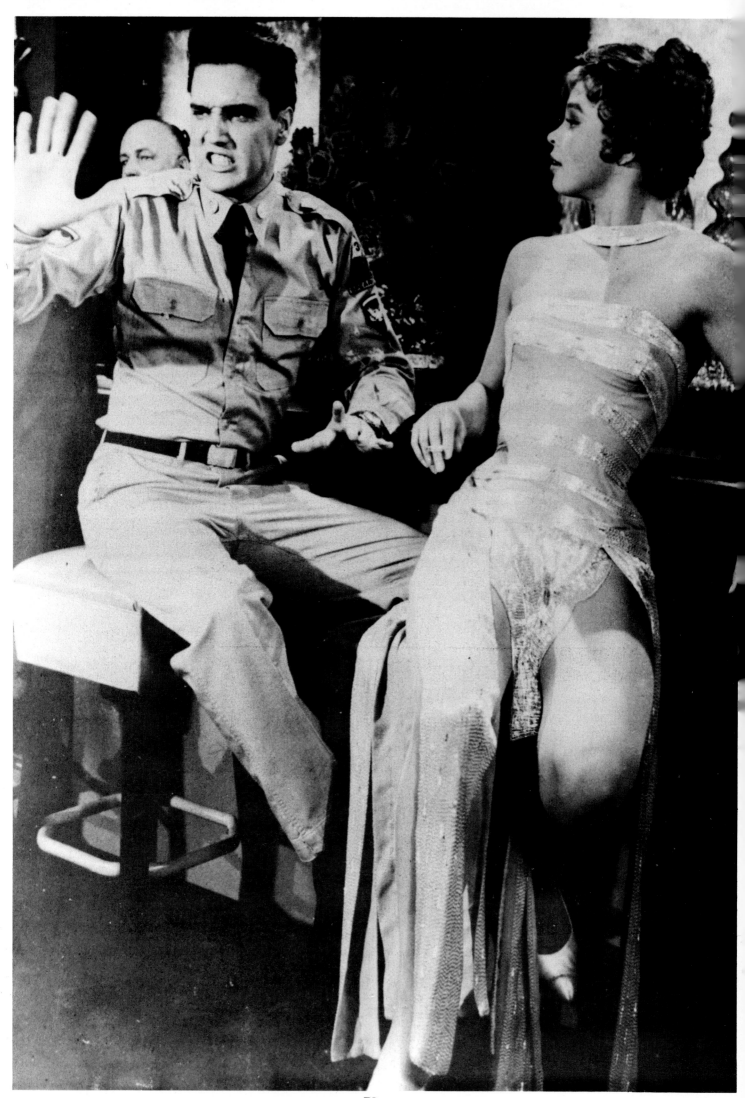

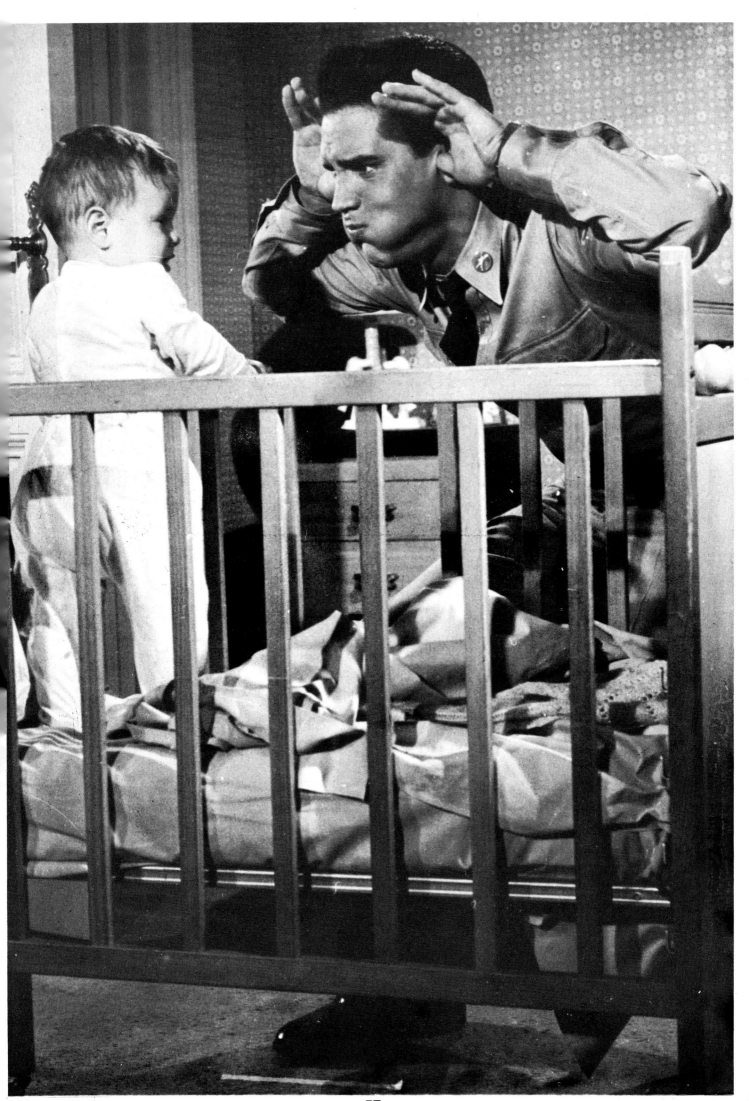

58

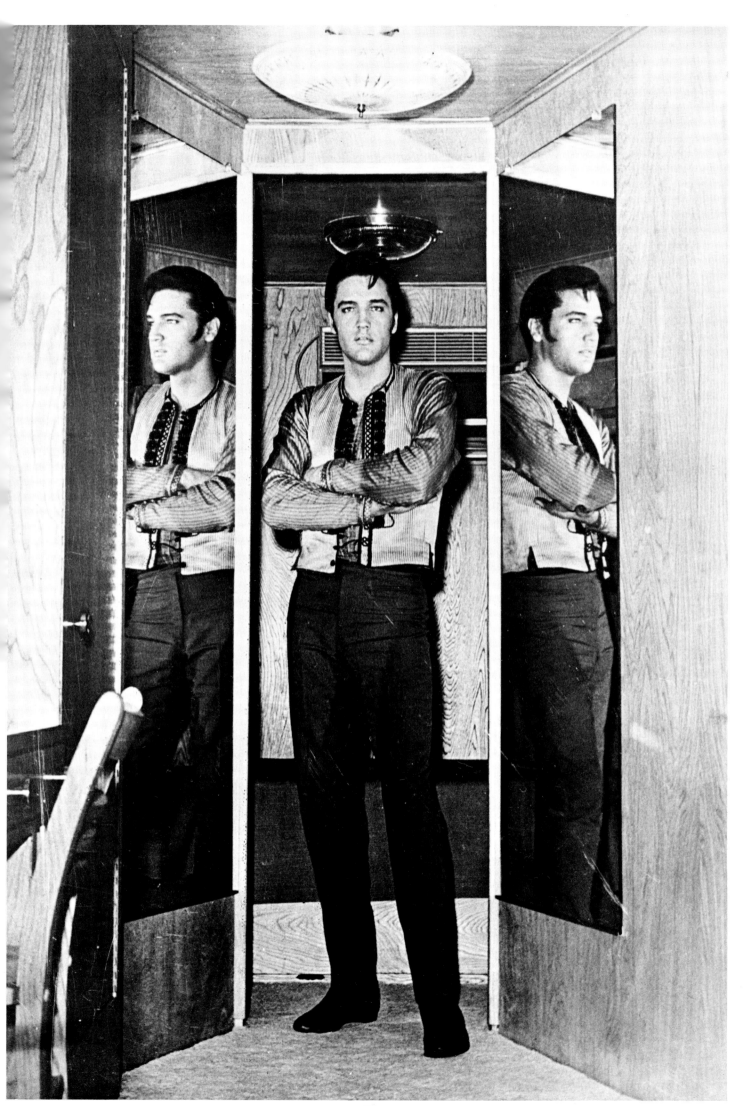

MARK ONE TRAVEL

Elvisly Yours

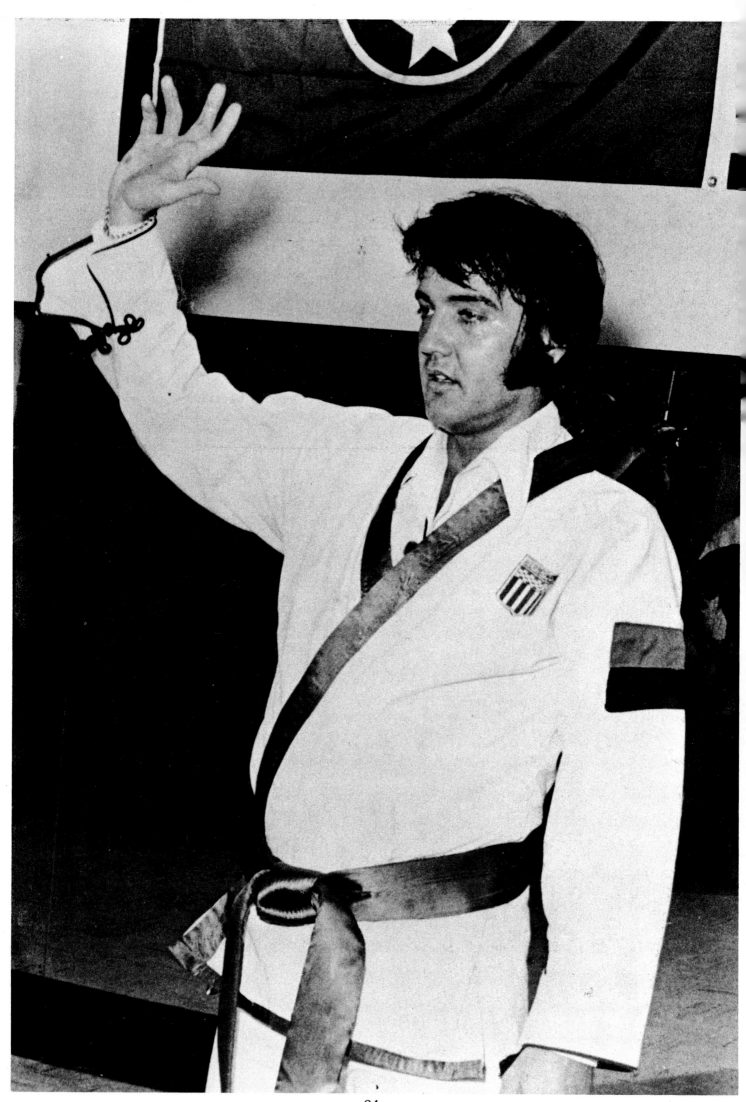

To My Friend Sid Shaw
Mayor Bill Morris
Memphis Tenn
1987

Shelby County Government
William N. Morris, Jr., Mayor

September 10, 1987

Mr. Sid Shaw
Elvisly Yours
P. O. Box 315
London NW 10, England

Dear Sid:

It was a pleasure to have the opportunity to visit with you in London during my recent trip as a member of the Memphis in May International Festival delegation. I appreciate your continued commitment to keeping the true story of Elvis Presley alive and I am grateful to you for the gifts of the two books, which were extremely good. Again, thank you for the gifts you and I hope that you can join us in Memphis next May as we celebrate the strong bonds between your country and ours.

Sincerely,

William N. Morris, Jr.
Mayor

WNM;Jr/sw

SUITE 850, 160 MID AMERICA MALL, MEMPHIS, TENNESSEE 38103